The Uncreating Word

ROMANTICISM AND THE OBJECT

The Uncreating Word

ROMANTICISM AND THE OBJECT

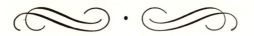

Irving Massey

INDIANA UNIVERSITY PRESS
Bloomington & London

PUBLISHED IN CANADA BY FITZHENRY & WHITESIDE LIMITED,
DON MILLS, ONTARIO

LIBRARY OF CONGRESS CATALOG CARD NUMBER: 77-126213
ISBN: 253-18993-4

MANUFACTURED IN THE UNITED STATES OF AMERICA

for
Arlene, Melez, Ephraim, James, Minou

Contents

Acknowledgments

I SHOULD LIKE TO THANK Albert Cook and Lionel Abel for reading the whole of this work in manuscript and for numerous bibliographical and stylistic suggestions which have improved the texture of the book to the extent that I have allowed it to be improved. Art Efron and Taylor Stoehr also read portions of the manuscript and did their best to strengthen its structure.

A practical debt of gratitude is due to the Graduate School of State University of New York at Buffalo, which provided a research grant that enabled me to examine Chateaubriand manuscripts in France and covered clerical expenses.

Symposium and *Queen's Quarterly* have kindly allowed me to reprint, respectively, "Subject and Object in Romantic Fiction" and "An End to Innocence," which had appeared in a different form in their pages.

The Uncreating Word

ROMANTICISM AND THE OBJECT

1

Introduction

THIS BOOK CONSISTS OF four essays, three of them with a common theme that is immediately apparent, the fourth intended to define the orientation suggested by the previous chapters. The first three essays contrast the attitudes found in a body of prose writing (mainly fiction) from about 1750 to 1850 with attitudes expressed or implied in Camus' *L'Etranger*. In the second chapter, *L'Etranger* is taken as the mirror image of *Don Quixote,* and the attitude usually described as "romantic" is situated at the intersection of the two perspectives. The third chapter, on the descriptive style, begins with Chateaubriand and Rousseau, one of them attentive to the objects of description, the other withdrawing from them into the self, and concludes with Meursault's sense of reality, which seems to occupy the reverse of what one might call the phenomenological ground, in which the objects are the self. In the fourth chapter, innocence is described in three categories: positive, negative, and neutral, with *L'Etranger* again serving as the example for the last. Chapter five (the title chapter) treats the question of the crisis in language, of which *L'Etranger* is symptomatic, as a consequence of the language-object relationships which developed in the nineteenth century.

3

At the historical level, the book (as the last chapter shows) is an attempt to follow out the movement from Sterne and Wordsworth toward unnamability and beyond. Dissatisfied with language, these authors resort to gesture or speaking silence; eventually, in a writer such as Camus, expression itself becomes a kind of mutism. The evolving confrontation between Romanticism and objectivism has as its by-product an increasing distrust of language. This hostility to articulation, leading to the concept of unnamability, eventually reverses itself, as reality (as Eros) reveals itself and demands a name.

At a more subjective level, these essays have a more Utopian purpose. They all seek a way back to a place where words and experiences are one, where ideas can resume their rightful place among things, and where problems can be solved not merely by posing other problems. The opposition between subject and object that dominates the first three essays obviously reflects this preoccupation, and the fourth essay is a rather elegiac review of the situation. The identical issues work their way through the details of these essays in a less obvious manner. The first, although originally conceived as a paper on Romanticism, deals not so much with period concepts as with the refusal to articulate, the ethics of silence, the defence of the ideal by the avoidance of statement in Vigny, in Tiutchev, in Camus; and this concern is a product of a contrary conviction: that there must be a time and place when an idea, even when spoken, is not a lie.[1]

The second essay is also close to the main theme. In questioning what categories can govern experiences where no categories can follow; in rejecting both geometry and concepts as instruments for the analysis of descriptive art; in opposing the total lie of criticism, it follows the first essay in repudiating the attitude towards the language-reality relation promoted by the enchanters of Cervantes, the false priests of Blake, and the judges of Meursault, all of whom would persuade us that to lie methodically is to be objective about spiritual experience.

The third essay in its very title ("An End to Innocence") expresses the sense of loss that the entire book reflects, and the implicit belief that a recovery is possible. It deals less with explicit or abstract statements about words and things and more with plot or action than the first two essays, but the principle of innocence is the same and can be extended to the other cases. For language too an innocence can be conceived in some pre-linguistic moment before thought has become word in the public sense and therefore lie and disprovable. In its inception word is wisdom, radiant before its birth into the world of equalization of all words. All words are privileged in their birth and become commonplace only as they are emptied into the ocean of neutrality.

Finally, the relation of the last essay to these issues is self-evident from its title, "The Uncreating Word."

My choice of *L'Etranger* as a device for bringing many of these problems into alignment may be regarded as anachronistic. It is obvious that the preoccupations it implies have been more sharply focused since, perhaps entirely transcended; in current terms *L'Etranger* is a primitive work, both on its own grounds and in the light of its own pretensions. But there is an advantage in using it rather than something of Robbe-Grillet's or any recent novel with similar concerns; it may be just as well to catch the concept of objectivism before its plunge into a sophisticated medium in which it becomes difficult to keep in sight the threshold from which it departed, the point where the word left the brink of experience: we become more preoccupied with its subsequent voyagings.

Certainly, to posit the problem in terms of a contrast between *L'Etranger* and various other works presupposes the perhaps mistaken acceptance of a philosophical scheme dominated by subjects, objects, and categories, even if only with the ultimate purpose of transcending such divisions. In a strictly phenomenological setting, for instance, many of the questions raised would not even be asked in the first place. In fact, to embark upon a literary discussion in which terms such as subject and object are taken seriously gives one the feeling of being in an obsolete milieu. It is true that the concept of "object," by itself, is still persistent in aesthetic theory; [2] but the pairing of subject with object is regarded as naive, and any opposition of the two flies in the face of the dominant philosophies of our century. Some linguistic philosophers would argue that the concepts of subject and object are not functions of our logic but only functions of our language.[3] For phenomenology, in which perception is less a relation than an act, a percept is a field of force, a crucible of stresses, rather than a given reality reflected in a subjective screen. For existentialism, at least as represented by Heidegger, the subject-object relation is an untenable, not to say ridiculous, metaphor; [4] Heidegger dismisses the Kantian *a priori* subjective principle with the simple observation that we cannot under any circumstances conceive of a subject that is initially worldless, subsequently reaching out towards a "world." [5] I am not aware that the structuralists have as yet assumed a definite position on this issue, though their implied attitude is fairly clear, but they are not likely to fall back into this ancient dichotomy when they do formulate an opinion. Yet literature, which sometimes lags behind philosophy, still lends itself to exploration in these terms, partly because it has itself been framed until recently on the presuppositions of the Platos, the Lockes, the Kants, or their opponents. I believe that a provisional, or even heuristic use of the subject-object formula can still yield useful insights into literature, and hope that though these insights may seem simple in the first essay, the method will have justified itself before the end of the book.

Granted, then, that my use of *L'Etranger* as a touchstone implies a certain philosophical as well as literary naïveté, I still find it curious that the same kinds of formulae seem to emerge once more from the very midst of a type of discourse which claims to leave behind the simple antitheses of realism and idealism. Robbe-Grillet criticizes Camus for remaining bound to his subjectivity while pretending to have devoted himself entirely to objects; yet he himself reverts to the most conventional opposition of subject and object when he declares that the trip during which he tried to identify the original sea-mews that he had described with such terrifying objectivity in *Voyeur* was, at least for that purpose, a waste of time; that these birds had no objective existence: their reality lay only in his own mind, and the supposedly "real" *mouettes* had nothing whatever to do with those in his book.[6]

Of course, thoughts and things are related not only by confrontation, but laterally as well; in the states of mind that precede articulation, or in reverie, thoughts and things sip at each other's frontiers, drain a common fund. The opposition of the two seems artificial.[7]

A similar objection (that the argument is being generated by assumptions, such as the subject-object distinction, that are not necessarily true) may be raised to the campaign against categories and conceptual schemes implicit in most of this book and explicit in the essay on the descriptive style. Perhaps if I had not assumed that abstract categories are the normal channels to the description of experience, I would have felt less need to contest their domination. It may be that the clash of perceptual judgments that leads to the suspense of metaphor, the conflict of perceptions that is our method of feeling our way around our world, is our customary way of knowing, rather than the simple observation of identities, with its usual corollary that when things fall into the same class, the non-entity they share is their principal ingredient of reality. I can only say that I hope with respect to this question my assumptions are indeed mistaken.

The border between a logic and linguistic theory is difficult to define, and a discussion of ways of thinking drifts almost necessarily into a discussion of language. The relation of subject and object is repeated in the problematics of word versus experience. It may seem odd to speak of that relation as an opposition, but an overvaluation of our expressive function and a minimization of our role as passive receptors has in fact forced the two into a hostile contrast. It is one thing to accept nominalism as an unfortunate but inescapable limitation on our human abilities; that proves the weakness rather than the power of language; it is another to try to transform it into a positive doctrine that would supplant philosophical idealism.[8] Words may be all that we can know in the end, but surely they are not all that we want or need to know. What we try to know, the field in which our effort to know takes place, is not merely the verbal field. If there were not a non-conceptual component in our experience there would be no percepts, only concepts. It may be true, in Strawson's phrase, that "we lack words to say what it is to be without them";[9] still, words cannot take the whole place of things, of that element in life that does not consist simply of our freely contributed conceptualizations. It is as though neither artists nor critics any longer believed in the component of passivity in our experience or in human suffering (in the sense that suffering is something imposed that one *has* to endure) or in the sobriety of true experience, but stir up a lather of words that substitutes oral activity and oral stimulation for the knowledge of what has happened to us in life.

Words as they have been used in the past were not, contrary to the claims of the current mode, attempts to conceal experience, but (as I have said) reflective statements of things that had really happened to us in life—not abstractions or falsifications. Now it is not permitted to record—only to create an experience every time one uses words—never to have an experience before one goes into verbal motion.[10] Perhaps the domination of the very young has set the fashion for this way of thinking—having no necessary, imposed experiences to draw on that have been forced on their awareness, they think they can create experience with words. But the fact is that life just *is*—we don't make it up each time we talk. We do not dictate it or merely project it; there is something there to begin with. The truth of our passivity, of our unstructured passivity, is being lost. (A symptom of this state of mind is the generally accepted critical cliché that every form of artistic realism is merely a convention.)

The dominance of words over experiences, of expression over the recording of what has really happened to us (and perhaps reality in this sense is only a function of the past) leads in turn to the dominance of concepts over experiences. In the process of looking for a word one must grope in the matrix of thoughts and things, the distinction of the two realms must be denied: words do not lead directly to other words without traversing experience, or at least without going back through that reservoir of language where the distinction between words and experiences does not pertain. It is not surprising that some authors should evince a distrust of language (see George Steiner's *Language and Silence*) when words are being made to support a weight they cannot possibly bear, by being required to invent their own reality. Words as used now often seem to refer to nothing—or indeed (*pace* Saussure) only to each other. But to deny words referential substance is to pretend that one has never seen, and to suggest that an interpretation is the only thing one reacts to in a work of art is to say almost the same thing.[11] In responding to a work of art, one is responding to its object, not to itself; one is incidentally retracing the process of interpretation, but only in order to grapple with the object. To remain blocked at the level of interpretation is to remain in the realm of anxiety that prevents experience in the first place and that would have forbidden the artist's eye to merge with its object, keeping him in the pale of his own concerns and reasonings.[12] To think before seeing makes seeing difficult, if not quite impossible. The mind is obstructed, not led, by concepts that move too rapidly into the path of experience. But even in the very moment when one looks at a landscape and sees only concepts, even when thought interferes with contemplation, the scene is telling one all the time from beneath that it is not really being blocked: it is asserting the quality of seeing in defiance of the act of thinking or structuring. The mind is not made only for concepts; it is also made to follow the movement of trees into mountain peaks.[13]

The dominance of concepts over experiences, as I have tried to phrase it, is nowhere more apparent than in criticism of the arts. Susan Sontag's "Against Interpretation" made the point some time ago, but it will bear frequent repetition. Criticism, whether good or bad, is only doubtfully related to the art of literature that it concerns, and the assumption that the abstract structures it recovers from a work of art represent what is most important in that work is mere infatuation. Perhaps, in fact, every achieved work of art is merely the reflex of a *failed* idea. Yet the usual approach to the analysis of literature is to look for concepts, whether expressed directly or implied by the "form"; and the alternative is a geometric method that hardly seems more adequate (see Chapter 3). Between them, neither will do; kinetic or geometric descriptions, using terms such as balance, direction, or form, are inert demonstrations that fail to explain why one kind of arrangement should be merely an arrangement, whereas another is of moment to us; and a conceptual interpretation, "insight," or idea about a work of art, no matter how dazzling it may seem at first, no matter how obliquely it reveals the secret set of an author's mind, usually clings for a while and then drops off, proving eventually that although it may be interesting in itself, it has no inevitable relationship with the work that occasioned it. To shift the ground of the problem to the audience, and find the specific artistic effect through a study of response rather than of stimulus, elaborates the problem without diminishing its basic difficulty.

The search for a structure in a work of art usually ends as a search for ideas: but having found the ideas, we have found nothing that tells us what makes this particular production a work of art rather than an argument. We are left only with the pretence of having discovered a key to its effect. If we wish to be honest, we do better to say nothing at all; in some way, we stay nearer to the truth if we adopt a mutist position in the manner of Meursault. As I have said before, to be objective about literature is not to tell lies about it, no matter how objectively the lies may be framed.

To get back to the area of Susan Sontag's discussion in "Against Interpretation": we do in fact seem to be heading towards a last day of criticism. There are no longer bodies of literature that raise questions, there are only approaches that produce topics. Nor does any given work suggest the method by which it should be studied; rather, the method creates the subject to be studied, as the cyclotron creates the new particle to be identified and described. Furthermore, a work is now numerically overpowered by the exponents of an idea. No sooner does a critical method emerge, be it phenomenology, structuralism, or McLuhanism, than it is put into practice by innumerable users. Where previously an idea was launched by a few critics and developed gradually by its followers over a period of time, the whole

of literature must now yield up its soul to the new interpretation within hours—the whole tradition has been
scanned and reformulated as phenomenological, formulaic,
structuralist, topological,[14] or whatever, overnight. The process is immediate and total. Now we are no longer approach-
ing literature, we are past literature. The critics continue
to swarm over literature, but it is either too soon for them
or too late. To paraphrase Kierkegaard, either we have now
really proven that literature can never be analyzed, or we
have proven that it has already been analyzed. We no longer
need to wait for methodological innovations to penetrate the
critical tradition—they simply convert it at once. Here perhaps McLuhan is right about qualitative change resulting
from quantitative, in this case from the number of critics
and instantaneous availability of their results, from their
sheer speed in processing ideas.

If the total achievement of a critical method is complete
within so brief a period, what do we do next? If there is no
need to pursue laboriously the illusion that a new idea may
lead us to final understanding, but literature yields its new
reading immediately? It becomes necessary to cast about
ceaselessly for new methodologies as the old ones are ex-
hausted; one must drop a work immediately to look for a
new methodology which will alter one's center of interest in
the work before that interest has developed a center—or
even alter one's choice of works to dwell on before one has
dwelt on one. One must reinterpret before the first interpretation has jelled; and so one has finally proven that the first
interpretation was only an interpretation and not the work
itself. That is, we see at last that even if we had remained
preoccupied with the work, we would only have been preoccupied with an interpretation. Now we are forbidden that
naïveté and can rest with neither "the work itself" (whatever
that may mean) nor the categories through which we first
apprehended it. It is no wonder that structuralism has ex-

perienced such a vogue; the bones start to show before the flesh, the structure before the substance. There is no substance, there are only structures; there are no works, there are only ideas about works. In such an atmosphere, a total equalization of importance comes about; no work of art is any longer of any importance, and the banality of intellectualized beauty comes to equal the banality of evil.

It is apparent that this introduction, in addition to summarizing the main ideas of the book, has involved another process. As I reviewed the material, I found myself looking for some center around which the obsessive concern with the unity of subject and object, language and reality, expressed in these chapters, revolved. No doubt it is a questionable procedure to try to think behind one's own thoughts, to look for a principle that organizes one's conscious preoccupations; for if one discovers such a principle and articulates it, it becomes merely one more in the series of subjects and loses both its binding force and the superior power of a latent or implicit idea. It then appears in turn only the emanation of some deeper thought. The only justification I can offer for this attempt to husk my own mind is that the kernel seems to be *latency* itself, as a kind of first cause or *Ding an sich* that does not submit itself for further analysis or ask for reduction, subdivision, or resolution into lesser entities. Perhaps generating, but not participating in, the subject-object, language-reality antinomies, it does not join the parade of "topics" as one more thing to think about, and it does not translate into the familiar coinage of neutral intellectual discourse. It is a point of departure which, especially in this book, would remind one that it is a terminus as well.

2

Subject and Object in Romantic Fiction

IT WILL BE APPARENT from the introduction that this book is not concerned with period concepts as such. It does not seek to establish the features or characteristics of any "movement" in order to contrast them with those of another. The contrast observed is rather between two points of view, one exemplified by a body of prose drawn largely from the early nineteenth century, the other by the works of Camus. By using the second to define the characteristics of the first I hope to suggest a way back to their reconciliation, or at least to an awareness of their once having been in the same place.

The first problem that *L'Etranger* helps us to identify in the body of earlier works with which I shall be comparing it is the role of physiological psychology in the development of an anti-romantic attitude. Materialist psychology was an important forerunner to the object-oriented philosophy of much contemporary literature. This philosophy is admittedly ambiguous; a preoccupation with objects can result as readily from the phenomenological bias that derives from Berkeleian idealism,[1] with its emphasis on particulars, as

14

from a straightforward mechanism; but for the present we shall concern ourselves with the latter strain.

The progress made by the science of psycho-physiology during the early nineteenth century helps to explain the uneasy attitude of many authors of the time about absolute ideals. What confidence could be mustered in an ideal which had been proved to consist in the hyperactivity of a patch of nerve tissue under a particular bump on the skull? To take one example: Alfred de Vigny, heralded by textbooks as a dyed-in-the-wool idealist, betrays on close reading the profound influence of the psycho-physiologists. In the manuscript of *Cinq-Mars* we find him declaring that the soul is merely a secretion of the brain whose existence terminates with that of the body. He concurs in the theory of physiological determinism which absolves the criminal of moral responsibility, declaring him to be a mental invalid or the victim of his congenital defects; above all, he seems to accept the materialist thesis of the phrenologists, whose attempt to localize the various faculties in compartments of the brain furnished a strong impetus to the development of behaviorism. Vigny's work is shot through with ideas from the eighteenth century sensualists, La Mettrie and Condillac, the Idéologues, and the phrenologists.[2]

Information relating to the influence of neurology on literature accumulates quickly under the eye of an attentive reader. Georg Büchner, physician and playwright, is obsessed with the apparent irrelevance of consciousness to the functions of the human automaton. Dostoyevsky, in *The Devils,* is concerned with the same issue of criminal responsibility vs. neurological determinism mentioned above.[3] Not even *War and Peace* remains aloof from the contemporary controversy over materialist psychology.[4] If we look hopefully further down the century, beyond the heyday of cerebral localization, we will still not find neurology dismissed and idealism suddenly revalidated. Synaesthesia, a literary theory presumably tending to undermine the phrenological claim that the mind can be mechanically compartmentalized, turns out to be all too obviously grounded in physiology, optics, and acoustics.[5] By the end of the nineteenth century the subtlest manifestations of mind were being hunted down to their crypto-cranial lairs, and not all the contortions of Gestalt psychology and psychoanalysis could nullify the accumulation of behavioristic facts. Today the discoveries of Penfield on the localization of memory, and the now commonplace technique of controlling mood and behavior through electrodes, continue to keep materialist psychology comfortably abreast of its philosophical rivals, such as neo-Husserlian phenomenology. Its broadest consequences are now apparent; but it was in the late 1700's that the climate of mechanistic relativism began to develop which eventually enabled us to accept as normal our lack of sense of direct contact with reality. What is more serious, in the context it provided, the very attitude of mind in which reality is sensed immediately in all its density, richness, and fullness of presence was demoted, becoming just one of the many possible states of mind on the same level of importance as the others, without claim to primacy or inclusiveness.

Although the physical study of the mind was not far advanced in the eighteenth century, systematic subjectivism in psychology consonant with what has been termed pre-Romanticism is even rarer, in the age of Hartley, than the equivalent in the nineteenth century. Godwin's chapter on the human mind in *Political Justice* does place considerable emphasis on the irrational and so constitutes one of the few exceptions of which I know. But even here a Byron or a Chateaubriand could have found only meagre pickings. True, in his introduction Godwin declares, after the manner of Vauvenargues,[6] that "The voluntary actions of men are under the direction of their feelings. Reason is not an inde-

pendent principle . . ." [7] There is also a remarkable awareness of the unconscious level of the psyche,[8] a level which
remains continuously active in the intervals of conscious
mentation (I, 413). The function of the intellect in the production of dreams is recognized as an actual unconscious
activity (I, 420), for Godwin assumes that neither volition
nor consciousness is a prerequisite for organized thought (I,
420). There is an adumbration of Gestalt in his cluster-
theory of perception (I, 406), in opposition to the prevailing
linear theory, together with a recognizable facsimile of Proustian memory (I, 411) and Bergsonian time.[9]

Godwin appears to hover on the fringes of those modern
psychological approaches that have sought to salvage subjectivity from the encroachment of the leucotome and the
electrode. Actually, his thinking is a little less revolutionary
than it may at first appear. Godwin's "unconscious" is not a
product of repression, but simply arises from the incapacity
of consciousness to cope with the plurality [10] and the fre-
quency [11] of its impressions. It is defined by the subtraction of
memory from thought (I, 411–412).

Godwin's sources do not appear to have been studied very
closely,[12] but Diderot's *Encyclopédie,* in the interesting entry
under the heading "Songe," does duplicate some of Godwin's
ideas. The article is drawn from the *Essai sur les songes* of
Jean-Louis-Samuel Formey, the secretary of the Berlin Acad-
emy (which seems to have encouraged the development of
subjectivist psychology). However, the common ground for
all of these is probably simply Leibnitz' *Nouveaux Essais sur
l'entendement humain.*

Struggling to preserve the soul from the inferior role of
accessory to the body, Leibnitz, like Godwin,[13] insists that the
soul has its separate existence, parallel to that of the body
but not finally dependent on it (*Oeuvres philosophiques,* I,
352). Hence the soul is always active, and consciousness is
only one of the phases of thought (Leibnitz, I, 77–78; see

also Godwin, I, 413, 404). "Ainsi il est bon de faire distinction entre la *perception,* qui est l'état intérieur de la
monade . . . , et l'*aperception* qui est la conscience, ou la
connaissance réflexive de cet état intérieur, laquelle n'est
point donnée à toutes les âmes, ni toujours à la même âme."
(I, 725). "Nous ne sommes jamais sans perceptions, mais il
est nécessaire que nous soyons souvent sans aperceptions."
(I, 124). Unconscious thought is not only a fact (I, 81) but a
necessity (I, 82–83). Furthermore, it is largely responsible
for both our habits and our opinions (I, 80), not to mention
our apparently unpremeditated actions (I, 80), and it deter-
mines the very quality or texture of our experiences, giving
rise to that "inquiétude . . . qui fait pourtant souvent notre
désir et même notre plaisir, en lui donnant comme un sel
qui pique." (I, 22).

As we stand with Leibnitz on the back doorstep of the
eighteenth century and look back over the seventeenth, we
begin to see the battlefield where our problem takes its rise,
between Lockean empiricism and Cartesian rationalism; the
one attempting to force the soul into the subordinate role
of a flickering accessory of physiological forms, the other
insisting that the action of the soul is indivisible and continuous, persisting through life and death, through consciousness and dreamless sleep alike. In fact, it is a keystone
of the Cartesian argument that man always dreams.[14]

When we shift our inquiry from logic to literature, all
our problems reappear; and not only reappear, but leap out
in three dimensions. The questions of criminal responsibility, of the border between rational behavior and insanity,
of the primacy of soul or body, are all involved in an appraisal of the Doctor's judgment on the sleepwalking Lady
Macbeth: "More needs she the divine than the physician."
If we set this line of Shakespeare's doctor beside a remark of
Vigny's Docteur Noir, we find a contrasting attitude, but the
issue is presented in the same terms. "Les médecins jouent

à présent dans la société le rôle des prêtres dans le moyen âge. . . . L'abbé a cédé la ruelle au Docteur, comme si cette société, en devenant matérialiste, avait jugé que la cure de l'âme devait dépendre désormais de celle du corps." [15]

Apparently inert abstract questions, such as whether there can be absolutely dreamless sleep, recur in literature as a struggle over values and the norms of reality. In the background of the mockery to which Don Quixote is subjected we can recognize the attack upon those who believed in the pervasiveness and continuity of dream and daydream by the exponents of a soul with only intermittent and strictly conscious functions. The vision of Don Quixote in the cave of Montesinos and Sancho's rhapsody on the seven little she-goats in the sky are to be taken seriously if the mind's unconscious work has substance, but may justifiably be laughed to scorn if the sole criteria of meaning and reality are physical mass and metrical extension. And if nothing but rational consciousness matters, then the fantasy is adequately employed when generating the shoddy hypocrisies of the false pastoral, the cynical masque, the disguises of the scoundrel Gines de Pasamonte, or any part of the nightmare would of the *dis*enchanters—in generating anything but the crusader's ideals in which the mad Quixote perseveres.

So far from irrelevant for the study of literature are the technical problems with which we began, that the reality of dream and the criterion of sanity have obviously been major preoccupations of great writers (Erasmus, Cervantes, Swift, Blake, Dostoyevsky) at least since the Renaissance; [16] while the stream of consciousness postulated by Leibnitz has persisted, both as moral purgative and literary technique, to the present day.

Let us turn from the general problem of the conflict between materialist and idealist psychology to the question of subjective and objective attitudes in Romantic literature.

The statement that *Don Quixote* prefigures most of the problems of Romanticism is a cliché. What is not so clearly recognized is that Romanticism can be understood as the middle segment in an arc of attitudes of which *Don Quixote* marks one pole and *L'Etranger* the other. In a word, Romanticism is the mid-ground between *Don Quixote* and *L'Etranger,* the intersection of the different ways of coping with life proposed by these two books.

The world of men sees only the physical exterior of Don Quixote; he, on the contrary, sees only its interior, its potential meaning, and persists in imputing values to it when the world itself acknowledges none. To the world Don Quixote appears absurd, because it perceives only his appearance and is blind to his significance; he seems a disordered machine, a puppet riding on a frame of sticks. His lack of meaning for other men is emphasized by his being made to act in a sort of puppet show, involving a real wooden horse, in the garden of the Duke and the Duchess.

In *The Stranger,* Camus has stolen a march on the materialists. He does not merely grant that absolute values are unattainable; he postulates the falsity of all subjectivity, of which values are only a special case. He disarms rationalist critics by creating a more objective character than they had ever dreamt of.

Meursault actually becomes a martyr to his objectivity. With absolute honesty, and with sublime indifference to the consequences of his honesty, Meursault rejects the demand that he censor his experiences or submit them to any preliminary evaluation. It is not even worth his while to save his life at the slight expense of describing his relationship with his mother in some conventionally acceptable way. In an objectivized world, where all ideals have been declared null and void, Meursault, the Stranger, can restore value to life only by keeping to the first level of inarticulate experience, entirely free from values. If all ideals are really false, reality becomes the one ideal worth disseminating. And so, in his own way, Meursault plays the Quixote for the modern world, the martyr and redeemer incomprehensible to mankind at large, refusing at the cost of his life to compromise to the slightest degree his ideal of experience uncontaminated by prefabricated generalizations. Don Quixote sacrifices himself for his ideals: Meursault sacrifices himself for the right to live without ideals.[17]

The Stranger, or rather the Outsider, is a pantheist. He has internalized the objectivity of the outside world. He has changed places with the windmill, and men try to force on him the spurious role of giant. Meursault is what the world took Don Quixote to be: an exterior without interior, a sort of human Möbius strip. From the angle at which the *récit* sets him, he seems to see himself with the same indifference with which the mountains regard him, and even to participate in their inner life. As Meursault gazes from his prison window upon the sky, one thinks of Shelley looking up at Mont Blanc, and wonders whether Shelley's problem has not found its answer in this strange new pantheism. ". . . Devant cette nuit chargée de signes et d'étoiles, je m'ouvrais pour la première fois à la tendre indifférence du monde. De l'éprouver si pareil à moi, si fraternel enfin, j'ai senti que j'avais été heureux, et que je l'étais encore."

The question whether one should define oneself as subject or object, the question whether the world itself is subject or object, is the gag that sticks in the throat of history halfway between Cervantes and Camus. Even Sterne's *Sentimental Journey* is a step in the direction of *L'Etranger*. Like the latter, it insists on an acceptance of every experience in succession without an evaluation or rejection of any one of them. Yorick refuses to humanize himself by the illegitimate device of fitting his experience into prepared categories. He is willing to forego the reader's sympathy, to admit that the play of random forces controls him as it does any physical *object,* in order to retain his integrity. Even the style of the *Sentimental Journey,* consistently declining to commit itself to emotion, with its remorseless accuracy and its refusal to draw conclusions, has something in common with the style of *L'Etranger.*

We learn from the *Sentimental Journey* that only by walking the tightrope of spontaneity [18] can one avoid falling into either sentimentality or coarseness. But whimsicality also becomes an excuse, an escape from the demand that we should be able to maintain permanent values in terms of real human relationships. The very fact that the ideal can be found only in the form of Maria the madwoman, with whom no relationship is possible, implies that only an abstract solution can be found to our problems, in an intermediate state that permits of no full involvement with another person. But even this half-emotion, or "sentiment," that Sterne so convincingly communicates, is extremely difficult to attain. It can be achieved only by withdrawing from personal love to an attunement with other individuals via the Great Sensorium; by avoiding the realm of direct relationships, where virtue and consistency count heavily, in favor of a plane where one's worst impulses can be understood not to nullify or contradict the existence of a soul; for this soul depends on its spontaneous honesty and not its unfailing virtue for the proof of its existence. Furthermore, a soul whose single undisputed value is honesty may not conceal either its material foundations or its uncontrollable evil impulses; and Sterne proves his soul's good faith by an obtrusive exhibition of both the latter.

During a famous scene, after drinking the health of the King of France, Yorick, in an expansive mood, feels an overwhelming impulse of generosity surge through him, so that " 'twould have confounded the most *physical précieuse* in France: with all her materialism, she could scarce have called me a machine—" (page 24). An elderly Franciscan enters, asking for alms; but after painting so affecting a portrait of the suppliant that the reader cannot refrain from participating in the author's generous impulse, Yorick declares flatly: "I had predetermined not to give him a single sous" (page 26). The explanation? In part, it is the fundamental irrationality of the human mind; more to the point, the passivity of the mind, which behaves like a material object in the grasp of physical forces. We have here an admission that man does have something in common with the *précieuses'* machine, after all. "No man cares to have his virtues the sport of contingencies" (page 25), but "there is no regular reasoning upon the ebbs and flows of our humours; they may depend upon the same causes, for aught I know, which influence the tides themselves." (page 25).[19]

A Sentimental Journey may be approached as well from the Quixotic side as through the perspectives of *The Stranger,* where value judgments are eliminated in order to preserve the authenticity of experience. Illusion too has its encomia in that book, juxtaposed with frequent reminders of the potency of material forces.[20] The Dulcinea theme also reappears, but in a reversed form. Although he has set out in search of what of beauty can be learned from women's souls (pages 120–121), Yorick often finds himself stumbling over their bodies. His journey through the new world of the Continent has been undertaken in the hope of finding whole-cloth emotion, but mere physical lust keeps getting in the way. He can accept a relationship only with Maria or with the absent Eliza, with neither of whom full intimacy is possible; in other words, he can accept only Dulcinea. Each passing episode involving a woman begins with sentiment, moves quickly into equivocation, and ends in crudity, as though Aldonza Lorenzo lay just beneath the skin of every woman in Europe. In order to rescue their character Yorick must withdraw before the fatal moment and perform the act of alchemy achieved by Don Quixote when he reinvested the whores at the inn door with their chastity. The affront of brutal vulgarity always lurks beneath the integral feeling that Yorick is pursuing. Sterne is understandably unsure which is the more reliable thing: whether there is more chance of grasping truth securely by clutching after Maria's delinquent goat or by holding on to the passing chambermaid.

The double view is always in force; from one side everything looks ideal, from the other, terribly crude. We are reminded of Werther's suicide, first as envisaged by himself and then as it is actually seen by the spectators. The point remains, that no incarnation of an ideal may be attempted by even the "pre-Romantic" fancy; given a body, the ideal mocks us as a clod. It becomes the false Dulcinea whom Sancho had once conjured up, to the confusion of Don Quixote. The true Dulcinea, we have said before, must be like Maria, who is kept at arm's length by her madness. Maria evokes from Sterne the central theoretical passage of the book, on sensibility as the "great *Sensorium* of the world." Here we see that Sterne had felt Maria to be in particularly close touch with Nature. By virtue of her madness she can serve as a channel to that Sensorium, to cosmic sympathy itself. It seems to me that "sensibility" in *A Sentimental Journey* is best defined as sensation which is at the same time sympathy, and Sterne becomes either vulgar or "sentimental" in the pejorative sense only when his attempt to keep in tune with this very special mood is unsuccessful. Maria's sweetness and sadness, like the peasants' dance which follows, is imbued with a distinctly religious quality which Sterne seems to associate pantheistically with the "naturalness" of the sentiments involved. ("God tempers the wind, said Maria, to the shorn lamb," or, "I beheld Religion mixing in the dance.") But Yorick cannot live in the universal consciousness as successfully as Maria can, through her madness, even though he declares bravely after his encounter with her, "I am positive I have a soul."

The close connection between the peasants' religion and Maria's spirituality emphasizes the identification of "madness" and the "natural." It is as though the quality of naturalness is felt to be preserved only in insanity. The only remaining carriers of the ideal are those who have refused to compromise with the world lest they lose their spontaneity; but in order to retain that spontaneity they must be mad. Even Erasmus had recognized this problem, as is evident from the final section of the *Praise of Folly,* "Laus stultitiae ex autoribus."

The difficulty with these mad folk is that, no matter how attractive they may be, they are really mad, and so they cannot function as heroes. On the other hand, the intended heroes of the Romantic novel, being compromisers, also cannot be real heroes. They are always, and often tragically, aware of their own insufficiencies—as for instance Yorick, in *A Sentimental Journey,* or Petchorin, in *A Hero of Our Time.* The pattern or prototype for the encounter between the hero and the madman, which we have been discussing in Sterne, is the meeting of Don Quixote and Cardenio in the Sierra Morena. There the reader is put in a position to see the difference between true idealism and mere "selfish" madness, so to speak, through the confrontation; but in the later works our doubts of the heroes' authenticity alter the lesson which such meetings communicate. It would seem that the closest approach Yorick can make to the ideal is wiping away Maria's tears and his own with the same handkerchief; wiping the tears from his own face, and from the face of the impotent Ideal.

A Sentimental Journey is a strange and disturbing book, and its conclusion is no less distressing than the body of the text. Despite appearances, it closes not with a bray of

ribaldry but with a cry of doubt. It is almost a "Pourquoi? et hélas!" [21] that we are left with. What else can one
feel, when the effort to vibrate in unison with the Great
Sensorium of the world ends with such a raucous cadence? [22]

A Sentimental Journey situates itself readily midway between the problem proposed by *Don Quixote* and the solution tacitly implied by *L'Etranger:* we can preserve values
only by living without them. *Die Leiden des jungen Werthers*
is concerned with the same issues. Why is Werther's suicide
presented so idealistically on the penultimate page and
described in charnel-house terminology on the next and last?
Is his subjective view of his death as an apotheosis the cor-
rect one, or does he really sink to the level of the *object*
which at the end he appears to be, when we no longer see
him through his own eyes? The author's failure to provide
an answer for the reader creates a stasis, obliging us to withdraw from our involvement in this conflict between subjective and objective reality to a level where we must contemplate it without participation. It is a solution which consists
in asking a question of us. There is a noteworthy similarity
between the apparent anticlimax of *Werther* and the sudden
return to material standards and conventionality in the final
pages of *Don Quixote;* in both cases the reader is left with
the feeling, not of having been cheated, but of issues which
seemed settled having been thrown open to question again.
The same is, of course, true of *A Sentimental Journey.*[23]
   The conflict of the subjective and objective views, as is
well known, pervades the book: indeed, for the first part of
our discussion of *Werther* we shall be on almost too familiar
ground. "What is Man, that much-praised Demigod! . . .
when he rises in joy, or sinks in sorrow, is he not brought
up short in both, returned to cold dull consciousness, at that
very point where he hoped to lose himself in the fullness of
Infinity?" But elsewhere, after describing how he enjoyed

having near him a servant who had been sent to soak in the ambience of Charlotte, Werther cries out: "God forbid that you laugh about it. William, must it be a fantasy whenever we are happy?" The unreliability of apparently immutable emotions also worries Goethe as it had obsessed Sterne; the formerly inspiring beauty of the morning, in the latter part of the book, lies before Werther "like a little lacquered picture, and all that swooning delight can't pump a single drop of happiness up out of my heart into my brain, and the whole fellow stands in the face of God like a dried-up well, like a leaky bucket."

The familiar problem of deciding what meaning should be attributed to insanity recurs in several places. Werther protests when Albert dubs his suicidal impulses "mad." "You people always have to say: this is stupid, that's clever, this is good, that's bad! And what does it all mean? Have you ever figured out the inner significance of any action? Can you expound with certainty its causes, why it happened, why it *had* to happen in exactly that way?" But Albert does have an explanation for suicidal impulses: a man "who is carried away by his passions loses all awareness, and must be considered drunk or insane." This is the voice of one of those anti-enthusiasts who were soon to gain powerful allies among the physiological psychologists of the nineteenth century. But oddly enough, the next time he returns to the topic of suicide, Werther too begins to speak of it not as heroism but as disease: "I find it as strange to hear people say that a man who takes his life is a coward as to say that someone who dies of a malignant fever is a coward," for the potential suicide is merely an invalid.[24]

The Quixotic and the medical explanations of extreme emotionalism seem to be grappling for ascendancy in Werther's mind, and possibly in Goethe's, too.[25] But Werther's encounter with an indubitably full-fledged madman helps him to triangulate his own position with accuracy. This

young man, Heinrich, has gone mad for love of the same
Charlotte who is the focus of Werther's problems and is
wandering on the hillside in late November looking for
flowers for his mistress. Werther envies Heinrich, for the
madman can ascribe his unhappiness to an objective cause,
such as the absence of flowers on the hillside in November;
he need not face the fact, as Werther must, that in his own
disordered heart and "in your discomposed brain lies that
misfortune, from which all the kings of Earth cannot save
you." But, Werther cries in anguish, he himself cannot be
happy like the madman, for the rationalists have stolen his
faith in illusion from him; and his trust in illusion being
his single bond with God, he begs God to take him back,
for he cannot bear to live on in a world where God is silent
and will not intercede to prove His own validity:

> Did you, who made Man poor enough, have to give him
> brothers who rob him of that tiny possession, that frag-
> ment of faith he had in you, All-Loving One? . . . Father!
> whom I do not know! . . . be silent no longer! your si-
> lence will not sustain this thirsting soul—and would a
> man, a father, be angry, if his son, returning unexpectedly,
> threw his arms about his neck and cried out: . . . be not
> angry because I have interrupted the wanderings that you
> wished me to endure longer. . . . I am only happy where
> you are.

The madman, then, has been able to keep his faith in
God, that is, the impossible reality, while continuing to
live; but he can do so only at the sacrifice of his reason.
Werther envies him his simple idealism. Ordinary people,
those who live close to Nature, share this quality. The peasant lad who later proved the strength of his emotions by
murdering his rival had previously impressed Werther with
the unbounded sincerity of his devotion to his mistress. "So
this love, this faithfulness, this passion, is not just a literary

invention. It's real, and can be found in its present form, among that class of people whom we call unlettered and crude. We, the lettered, who have become nothing but letters." The implication that Charlotte is not the main-spring of his problems is hard to avoid,[26] for clearly Werther is himself one of those who are "nothing," who do not really invest their faith in any actual person or thing.

Werther also envies Albert his devotion to his work; but he would not be happy in Albert's place, for he lacks Albert's ability to find value in real things. What Werther suffers from is not an excess but an insufficiency of the poetic im-pulse, of the readiness to idealize, to attach a mythical value to simple reality. His loss of interest in Homer after his fail-ure to become involved in real life seems symbolic of his loss of the mythopoeic faculty. The simple people in *Werther,* such as Albert and Wilhelm, are not merely Philistines, to be contrasted unfavorably with the hero. On the contrary, it is *they* who are idealized, even to the point of over-simplifica-tion; the only one whose mind is medically anatomized is the subjectivist Werther. The summary characterization of the others becomes quite unrealistic. Mrs. M., for instance, when we discover her upon her deathbed, is solely con-cerned with straightening out accounts with her miserly husband so that the fact that she has had to steal money from the till to keep the household going will not confuse her successor's reckoning. This deathbed transaction is the upshot of her thirty years of marriage.

Such a thumbnail biography, in its abrupt, almost drab practicality, reminds one that emotion is not necessarily directed towards the self, but may be invested entirely in the external phases of life. For this is the real fairytale in *Werther:* the myth that life can really be a practical thing, that life is comprehensible to and comprehended by some people. And because Goethe does not see how such a state is possible in reality, he poetizes and fictionalizes all the figures

who do devote themselves to life, while analyzing Werther
in realistic psychological detail. Mrs. M. is made to seem
capable of converting finance into fairytale. She finds the
justification of her death, and her victory over death, in her
meticulous honesty about money. All feeling has been given
over to money, the essence of the objective world. Mrs. M.
has reached the ideal by balancing the budget.

Mrs. M., and the other over-simplified characters like her
in the book, are successful people, for they can attach themselves to a symbol. They are perhaps more monomaniac
than the confused Werther himself. They can all do the
right thing when called upon to prove that they are com-
mitted to life—they can murder for love, go mad for love,
work for love—but they are not real people. Their char-
acterizations are scamped and summarized. Only Werther
himself, the failure, is the realist and the real person; the
others are psychological impossibilities.

In a curious way, then, the dull, blunt, practical pizzicati
that punctuate *Werther* bespeak more faith in the mythical
content of reality than do its marvellous lyrical rhapsodies.
Werther's suicide is a withdrawal and a confession that he
cannot commit himself to experience as the simple heroes,
the peasant, the murderer, and the madman can. For
Werther has had to imagine all the petty realities in the
book; he has no belief in an external reality to begin with
and has to invent it for himself. Only objective reality is
non-objective and unreal for Werther; therefore, these dull
or commonplace passages, which present his notion of the
external world, constitute the truly fantastic and entirely
"created" elements of the book. The Odyssean littleness of
the plain people is the expression of a faith in objective
things which he cannot achieve. Unable to approach this
mythically satisfying version of reality, he must invert himself and go inward to find some equivalent satisfaction in a
spiritual life beyond death. But the rather harsh ending

throws the success of even that endeavor into question. We have here, as was mentioned previously, a conclusion comparable to that of *Don Quixote;* Quixote admits defeat at the end, resigns his effort to find Dulcinea, and transports his virtues to a higher world, where the pursuit of the ideal cannot be invalidated by material evidence.

Before committing ourselves finally to the downward slope on which objective reality holds undisputed sway, we may pause to look for a plateau, or at least a resting-place. Trapped as we are in the logic of our own subject-object assumptions, there seems to be only one direction in which we can ultimately go. But even within this system there have at least been attempts at finding a balance of forces. I should like to explore one of these briefly, although it lies outside our period, as a preliminary to the discussion of an early nineteenth-century author, E. T. A. Hoffmann, who exhibits some elements of such a compromise.

Ramon Fernandez' analysis of the Impressionist style in *Messages* (1926) may be read as a transitional effort that helps to bridge the gap between Bergson and Robbe-Grillet in the aesthetic theory of the object. "It is certain," he says, "that the passage from self to non-self, perhaps the most important event in human life, does not take place initially through a distinct and clear intellectual act, and can be understood only through the presence in us of the 'confused perceptions of the universe,' to use Leibnitz's terms." [27] "The sketching in of an intuitive nature, intermediate between the reality and the idea, and comprising the essential principle of the latter, is the purpose of what has been called, broadly speaking, Impressionism." [28] Fernandez' wording recalls the strategy of Thomas Reid's reply to Hume during the eighteenth-century analogue to this controversy (see above, n. 9): the self is not discontinuous, because it does not apprehend experiences as a series of discrete entities like the words in a sentence, but in an immediate and comprehensive way that has nothing to do with the delays and the sequences of a linguistic pattern; perception reaches us whole, before the analytic machinery of language resolves it into series. "There is nothing like Impressionism," says Fernandez, "to make us apprehend experience in the moment of its generation, *before* the artificial control of percept and concept has set in . . ." [29] Fernandez envisages a process in which the object first strikes below the level of purposive consciousness, then is dissolved into the self, then is reconstituted by the active intelligence: "Regarding this dissolving of the object into our self as the first stage in a functional re-adaptation, it [Impressionism] understands that the second stage consists of a new affirmation of the object, based upon the 'given' of the first, passive experience." [30] The whole sequence is reminiscent of Nicholas of Cusa's theory of perception, in which the image itself is treated as proof, in us as it were, of our idea of the image. God is "the Samplar of all things. Therefore whereas the Samplar of all things shineth in the mind, as the truth in the image, it hath in it self, that where it looketh . . ." The mind "is like unto one that is a sleepe, untill it be stirred up by admiration, proceeding from sensible things, to be moved, then by the motion of its intellectual life, it finds described in itself that which it seeketh. But thou must understand, that this description is a resplendance or shining of the Samplar of all things, after the same manner that the truth shinneth in its image." [31] Compare Jean-Pierre Richard on the opposite process in Mallarmé: "In his case the inner adventure demands a *proof,* that can only come from the world of sense." [32]

It is tempting to linger on the balance and to cast about for other authors, contemporaries of Sterne and Goethe, who would enable us to hold our equilibrium between subject and object a little longer. But such tactics would be false to the impulse of our premises, and we might be accused of remaining at an impasse of our own creation. After all, one virtue of the subject-object philosophy is precisely that instead of dwelling in compromise it forces us to confront extremes. The only justification I can offer for prolonging our exploration of the "plateau" between subject and object with one more author is that the intermediate domain, neither quite heavenly nor worldly, in which E. T. A. Hoffmann pitches his region of security seeks to preserve us from extremes without loss of the intensity that only extremes can yield. In some parts of Hoffmann's work we retrace the paths that we have already traversed; but in this author there is also an area of ambiguity beyond polarities that is not merely the helpless vacillation of a Werther. A story like "The Golden Pot," in a conventional idealistic style, transports us to a world dominated by benign spiritual forces; "The Sandman" illustrates the effort to resist the demonic powers and achieve an ideal life in the real world, though it drives its hero over the brink of raging madness in the attempt. But in "Councillor Krespel" or "The Automaton" a solution is found, or rather several solutions are found, that allow the fullness of the transcendent impulse to find expression without dropping into the artifices of a Cockaigne or shattering against the dead-wall of reality.

Even "The Golden Pot," for all its fantasies, hints at the structure of an answer to the problem in its suggestion that there must be a unifying force behind antinomies. The country of Atlantis, to which the student Anselmus is transported, is, to be sure, a never-never land; but the kind of alternative offered by the materialist philosopher (Nicolai), in a notorious joke current among the German *literati* of the time, is even more improbable. When Anselmus speaks of his vision, in which he had seen three beautiful talking snakes, Dean Paulmann remarks (almost as Albert in *Werther* might do): "Oh yes, that is a physical ailment, which can be treated by applying leeches to the behind, *salva venia,* as a distinguished scholar, recently deceased, has shown." The crassly physical is as unreal as the ineffably ideal, for a reason that Hoffman only makes explicit elsewhere (in "Don Giovanni"); it is because both are notions or hypotheses rather than anything that is directly known. What is directly known is the spiritual life behind them both, which merely generates the notions of the ideal and the physical as polarities, but these have no self-subsistent existence. "The conflict of the divine and the demonic powers begets the concept of the earthly life, as victory in that conflict begets the concept of the supernal life." The truth lies in the ultimate force behind these conceptualizations, that pierces the papery surface of experience from time to time like a shaft of burning glass. Usually, in Hoffmann, these visitations occur in the form of music, and his musical stories reveal much more about this answer to the conflict of the ideal and the real than does "The Golden Pot"; but I shall return to those later.

Like "The Golden Pot," "The Sandman" contains some elements of the conventional opposition between materialism and idealism, but in a context psychologically so gruesome that no comfortable intellectual formula can reconcile them. Still, such a formula is suggested in the story, whether one can take it seriously or not. The student Nathanaël must choose between the merely human Klara and the artifact Olympia, who is nothing but a mechanism, a wooden doll. In the struggle of choice he goes completely mad. It may be that he must go mad because, given such a choice, one cannot help but go mad. Yet Anselmus in "The Golden Pot" was rescued from a comparable fate by his belief in the magical snake-girl Serpentina, and (this is the "formula" of which I speak) there are indications in "The Sandman" that Nathanaël could have attained the same salvation if he had been able to nurse the light in the uncanny Olympia's eyes to a steady flame. He goes mad as much because he has failed the challenge of the ideal as because he has not come to terms with the real. An analogy between Sterne's Maria and Nathanaël's not-quite-human beloved inevitably suggests itself here. Nathanaël cannot really speak to Olympia, any more than Yorick can enter into true communication with Maria; the second is a madwoman, the other a machine. The real communication between Nathanaël and Olympia, like that between Yorick and Maria, is but the sharing of a sorrow. The only words Olympia knows are "Ach!" and "Gute Nacht, mein Lieber!"; but they are enough to express what the whole story conveys: that this time, at least, the effort to bring the ideal to life will fail. A lament, and an elegy, they too recall the "Pourquoi?" and "hélas" at the end of Vigny's *Stello*.

As I have said, the "musical" stories of Hoffmann give us direct access to his solution for the conflict of the subjective with the objective. The penetrating intensity felt in Hoffmann's descriptions of musical effects has, to my knowledge, no match in literature. In stories like "Don Giovanni," "The Automaton," or "Councillor Krespel" the communication of a musical timbre through the fibrous matrix of words becomes at moments almost unendurably powerful. Councillor Krespel has been seeking the source of music in violins all his life. He dismembers the finest instruments for the purposes of his futile research; but the magic of the automaton, that seems to be the independent possession of some mechanical principle in the violin, is neither in its physical structure alone nor in any virtuoso manoeuvre one executes upon it, but in some searing power that lurks behind the instrument waiting to surge towards the being whose sympathy with that power is complete. The fate of Antonia, Krespel's daughter, is identical with that of Semele. Antonia may not sing, for the gift of her voice is not to be contained by any instrument, least of all the fragile instrument of the body, and when she does sing the instrument is shattered, together with the best of Krespel's violins.

When Antonia dies, Krespel need no longer probe the structure of musical mechanisms, and his riddle is solved. After some false starts, he has ridden the current of truth to its source. The beginning of music lies beyond life; with this knowledge, he need no longer try to seek it here. Music and person are the same; neither is *available* in life. This does not mean that life is bad; it is just a place where one can learn to discriminate the adventitious from the final, the earth-born from the divine.

What is it that has come together at the end of "Councillor Krespel"? What has clinched? It is not simply that the earth-born and the divine have finally been united through Antonia's death; rather in one sense they have been still more distinctly separated, as Krespel returns, both fulfilled and relieved, to his domain, and Antonia goes on to hers. Yet some two things have hit, in this most significant yet most enigmatic of Hoffmann's stories.

Without trying to give more of a name to Hoffmann's solution for the subjective-objective dilemma than the above outline of "Councillor Krespel" may suggest, I should like to go on to another tale, "The Automaton," in which the same issue presents itself in a different version. Here the question of the meaning of mechanism is raised fairly and explicitly. If man's aesthetic sense can be duplicated in mechanical instruments, is not man himself proven to be nothing more than a machine in that very area which we usually regard as peculiarly human? What is the meaning of an art produced by automata? One clear answer is offered in the story itself, by the character Ludwig: the creation of a mechanical instrument "is for me a declaration of war against the entire spiritual principle." But this remark is obviously a simplification and does not strike the truth anywhere near the centre, for in the same story we have already been treated to a magnificent concert by musical automata under the direction of Professor X, a concert which has had an undeniable spiritual impact. In a way, the mechanical music is an expression of the opposite of mechanism. Music, when real, is not our squeezed-out product but something that happens within us without our action; we are at most the instrument through which it emerges into sound, but we do not participate in its creation. If we participate we only interfere. It has to take shape itself, voiced by the force that is the speech within us. That force is also the tap from which thought and expression run—a thought that is never our thought but its thought. In this way the non-personal mechanical instrument or puppet is a truer expression of the independence of music from human production and conditioning than the human performer or composer can be. As Kleist put it in his famous tract "On Marionettes," "Paradise is barred and the Cherub behind us; we have to go all the way around the world and see whether it isn't open again somewhere in back." [33]

In the same story by Hoffmann there is another kind of robot, a mechanical Turk who answers questions that people put to him privily.[34] Again the mechanical is shown to be superior to the merely human, for the Turk answers the most important question that Ferdinand can ask him. This mere toy, this clockwork Turk, has an uncanny presence and authority. He is really his questioners playing on the instrument of their selves and bringing out through an objectification of their consciousness the awareness they have had only dimly before. He enables them to polarize and concentrate that ultimate truth that the self-within-the-self can tell them, as (Hoffmann says) a voice (not our voice yet ours) in dreams tells us what previously we only dimly knew.

The machine, automaton, or physical world for Hoffmann is an opportunity offered to us to reach the archetype in this world, the absolute detached from us that fulfills us, without our having to soar or sink. But, undeniably, though experienced within life, it points beyond life, and ultimately it draws us out beyond life as we know it. The last time Ferdinand sees his beloved, he will hear her sing. But the last time he sees his beloved, as the Turk has told him, she will die.

> Mio ben ricordati   s'avvien ch'io mora
> quanto quest'anima   fedel t'amò.
> Lo se pur amano   le fredde ceneri
> nel urna ancora   t'adorerò!
>
>   (Metastasio,
>   *Alessandro nel India*)

(My dearest, remember, if I should die,
How much this faithful soul once loved you;
And if cold ashes still can love,
In the urn I shall still adore you).

There is no withdrawal from the ideal at the end of a Hoffmann story, only a withdrawal from life.

A simpler and more direct sort of conclusion defines the outcome of Vigny's *Stello,* a work which marks the definitive abandonment of our difficult holding-ground between subjectivity and objectivity. The resignation from the pursuit of the ideal in this world, and the recognition that this search is appropriate only in another context, becomes in this book not a necessity imposed on the hero at the ultimate moment, as in *Werther,* or a realization that accompanies each moment of fulfillment, as in Hoffmann, but simply a prior assumption of experience; one might call it a prerequisite for living. Unlike *Werther,* for instance, this work makes it clear from the beginning that the game of life is not meant to be won; one must start by acknowledging that the best life (known now for some time, and in many senses, as the absurd life) is achieved by the abrogation of hope and by a steady recognition of the inevitability of sorrow.

The ideal which the poet Stello is making his misguided attempt to incarnate does not have the form of Dulcinea, Eliza, Olympia, or Charlotte, but rather bears some dim resemblance to Saint-Simon.[35] Nevertheless it draws him no less surely towards suicide or insanity for being a sociological chimaera rather than an amorous fantasy. The familiar problem of *Quixote* mounts once more to the central position; the faint border between idealism and madness is blurred, and the line which in Hoffmann has become almost indistinguishable must be retraced in the sharp black ink of Doctor Noir. *Stello* is the extended account of a psychiatric interview; it suggests that the cure for the hero's rampant fancy must come through the acceptance of his proper role among the other objects of the world. As for his ecstatic aspirations, they will simply not hold water in the age of phrenology; Dr. Gall's little devils can punch holes in every transcendental bump on Stello's skull. If absolute values are to be pursued at all, they must be sought only after death and out of this world.

A small but significant detail of *Werther* reappears in *Stello* with a startling corollary. Werther had blamed the rationalists and mechanists for robbing man of his faith; Vigny not only does the same, but attributes the madness of the poet Gilbert to the materialist polemic. Similarly, Blake had once claimed that Cowper had gone mad "as a refuge from unbelief—from Bacon, Newton and Locke." The *philosophes* drive poets to madness, which is the last refuge for their idealism; since there is no room for illusions in a rational world, the poets must build an irrational one in which to keep them. It is the familiar story of Peter Pumpkin-Eater, who, unable to make his wife stay at home in a conventional house, put her in a pumpkin shell; and there (or at least so the rhyme assures us), there he kept her very well. One can only add that the problem is complicated by the difficulty of being sure that the irrational house is any less rational than the rational one.

Stello has one alternative to the retreat into madness or suicide illustrated by Gilbert and Chatterton: that is, to become like Doctor Noir. Doctor Noir, like Camus in *L'Etranger* and Sterne in *A Sentimental Journey,* rejects all subjectivity as unreliable. The degraded Quixote, Stello, cannot raise his voice for one instant in defence of his aspirations without being riddled by the Doctor's sarcasm. If one is to harbor ideals and values at all, one must never articulate them. Doctor Noir is himself no cynical material-ist, but he is wise enough to know that any ideal, once enunciated, is vulnerable to the solvent of relativism. Better to acknowledge man's "Réisme" ostentatiously, better to emphasize the instability of his ideals and his enslavement by psychological determinism, if one hopes to ward off the evil eye of reason. Modern man, if he has faith at all, would rather hide it than parade it. "What is the idea that sustains his courage? He will not even say." Any values which he acknowledges must be immanent in experience and expressed only in action.[36]

Doctor Noir's final lesson is the lesson of honesty. Only by first acknowledging the dominion of the material elements in one's organization can one avoid becoming their victim. The value of honesty alone remains when all others have been liquidated; and this kernel of honesty is the germ of *L'Etranger.*

L'Etranger, alone among the books we have been con-sidering, does not have to end with an anticlimax or, like Hoffmann's stories, find an elaborate justification for a difficult faith. In the other texts, from *Don Quixote,* through *Werther,* to *Stello,* there is a willingness to grant that the idealist is potentially suspect if not absolutely wrong, that he may be of unhealthy mind and in need of a cure. At the same time the gap between the ideal and the real dwindles, until the ideal shrivels to a metaphor. Therefore the anticlimax, the return to the material world, is most painful in *Don Quixote;* it is mildest in the wistful "Pourquoi? et hélas!" of *Stello,* in which reality has never been left very far behind. Nevertheless, each book does end in tragedy or disappointment. But in *L'Etranger,* where man stands with matter at the level of the object, issues no manifestos which reality will fail to honor, and makes no demands of himself, there can be no reawakening and no disillusionment; for working out a position for himself within the external world of objects, rather than trying to rise above it, the outsider has nowhere to fall to. In his one-dimensional world, one does not go either up or down.

One may ask, of course, whether the reverse defence of the ideal in *L'Etranger* is successful. In one sense it is so, for the book can still be read; it continues to carry some force and some conviction. On the other hand, the tactic it employs, of embracing the objective to rescue the subject, conclusive and effective as it seemed in its own time, must now be seen as part of a continuing process rather than a terminus *ad quem.* *Don Quixote* and *L'Etranger* mark the extremes of attitudes which find their intersection in the group of works we have been studying, and this group of works is illuminated and brought into focus by being placed at that intersection for study. Still, of course, the problem which Cervantes and Camus try to solve in their opposite ways is there before and after. As we look back from Cervantes, we see that the larger issue of which this is a part, the relation of body and soul, whether stated in medical, philosophical, or literary terms, has worried modern culture ever since the humanists Marsilio Ficino and Erasmus first tried to cope with the danger that loomed in the Paduan practice of maintaining a sharp distinction between matters of reason and faith.[37] Looking forward from Camus, we see the approach adumbrated in *L'Etranger* followed through in many areas of our more recent culture. The mutism encouraged by Camus is reflected in the general withdrawal from both the written and the printed word advocated by poets, structural linguists, and philosophers of several schools. The thought seems to be that in speech the idea is absorbed into the speaker as soon as it is spoken and its authenticity cannot be challenged. It is, so to speak, swallowed for safety.[38] But this is an evasion of the issue: we cannot learn to use language creatively by not taking responsibility for what we say. Unrecorded and unrepeated speech does not provide a guarantee of authenticity just because written or printed words guarantee inauthenticity.

Similarly, the expectation implied in Camus' courageous if imperfect embrace of objectivity, that the arts can carry the unnamed creative component into the very heart of technology and conquer mechanism by absorbing the machine, seems to have been universally implemented, although for some of us an uneasiness remains. Aleatory techniques in music, the visual arts functioning as direct extensions of a model of the nervous system, reliance on drugs for aesthetic stimulation, the dissolution of identities and substitution of objects for people in the literary experience, all express the confidence that art can brook the direst threat of science. Undoubtedly art must proceed in this way to preserve its authenticity, and to some degree its current forms merely reflect the present structure of our consciousness. At the same time such tactics also expose the arts to a systematic intellectualization that brings them up to the plane of self-consciousness of technology but exiles them from the necessary ignorance of experience.[39] The enthusiasm for any mechanical artifice that can be forced into relation with art and for every philosophy that justifies this yoking bespeaks a persistent obsession with the threat of science, and a readiness to let science dictate the issues with which art will be concerned; it betrays a defensive attitude that makes the arts after all, in a more immediate sense than ever before, the dependents of technology. It may be that those refinements upon Camus' objectivism that now make *L'Etranger* seem an intellectually primitive work, though they appear to challenge the powers of materialism in the very midst of its camp, are at the same time oblique concessions to the demand that man revise his scheme of experience. They cast, however faintly, the shadow of a new book "Du vrai, du bien, et du beau," appropriate for an assemblage of objects, incidentally endowed with consciousness, that might still pass under the name of the human race.

3

The
Descriptive Style:

CHATEAUBRIAND, ROUSSEAU, CAMUS

My purpose in this essay is to define three approaches to landscape description in literature. I begin with Chateaubriand's because his is the most naïve and perhaps for that reason the most satisfactory. There are several kinds of nature description in Chateaubriand, but the set pieces of generalized pseudo-classic landscape of the kinds one finds scattered through *René* are not of immediate concern for the initial stage of my argument, though they will have relevance later; I wish to attend first to those passages in which Chateaubriand gives us the feeling that we are being immersed in a real landscape. For my purpose the famous description of the autumn birds in part I, book III of the *Mémoires d'outre-tombe* will serve well enough, although the passage is so well known that it becomes difficult to catch a fresh impression of it.

44

Plus la saison était triste, plus elle était en rapport avec moi: le temps des frimas, en rendant les communications moins faciles, isole les habitants des campagnes: on se sent mieux à l'abri des hommes.

Un caractère moral s'attache aux scènes de l'automne: ces feuilles qui tombent comme nos ans, ces fleurs qui se fanent comme nos heures, ces nuages qui fuient comme nos illusions, cette lumière qui s'affaiblit comme notre intelligence, ce soleil qui se refroidit comme nos amours, ces fleuves qui se glacent comme notre vie, ont des rapports secrets avec nos destinées.

Je voyais avec un plaisir indicible le retour de la saison des tempêtes, le passage des cygnes et des ramiers, le rassemblement des corneilles dans la prairie de l'étang, et leur perchée à l'entrée de la nuit sur les plus hauts chênes du grand Mail. Lorsque le soir élevait une vapeur bleuâtre au carrefour des forêts, que les complaintes ou les lais du vent gémissaient dans les mousses flétries, j'entrais en pleine possession des sympathies de ma nature.

Le soir je m'embarquais sur l'étang, conduisant seul mon bateau au milieu des joncs et des larges feuilles flottantes du nénuphar. Là, se réunissaient les hirondelles prêtes à quitter nos climats. Je ne perdais pas un seul de leurs gazouillis: Tavernier enfant était moins attentif au récit d'un voyageur. Elles se jouaient sur l'eau au tomber du soleil, poursuivaient les insectes, s'élançaient ensemble dans les airs, comme pour éprouver leurs ailes, se rabattaient à la surface du lac, puis se venaient suspendre aux roseaux que leur poids courbait à peine, et qu'elles remplissaient de leur ramage confus.

La nuit descendait; les roseaux agitaient leurs champs de quenouilles et de glaives, parmi lesquels la caravane emplumée, poules d'eau, sarcelles, martins-pêcheurs, bécassines, se taisait; le lac battait ses bords; les grandes voix de l'automne sortaient des marais et des bois: j'échouais mon bateau au rivage et retournais au château. Chateaubriand, *Mémoires d'outre-tombe* (III, xiii).[1]

The more mournful the season, the closer I felt to it; the rimy fall, making travel difficult, isolates the country dweller: one feels better sheltered from other people.

There is a moral quality in the scenes of autumn: these leaves that fall like our years, these flowers that fade like our hours, these clouds that flee like our illusions, this light that pales like our understanding, this sun that grows cold like our love, these rivers that freeze like our lives, have secret relations with our destiny.

I saw with inexpressible pleasure the return of the season of tempests, the passage of the swans and the doves, the gathering of the crows in the flats near the pond, and their settling at the coming of night on the highest oaks of the great drive. When the night raised its bluish vapour at the forest crossroads, and the complaints and lays of the wind moaned in the withered moss, I entered into full possession of the sympathies of my nature.

In the evening I would go out on the pond, steering my boat alone among the reeds and the large floating leaves of the water-lily. There the swallows would gather, ready to leave our clime. I did not miss a single one of their chirpings: the child Tavernier was less attentive to an explorer's tale. They would play over the water at the setting of the sun, chasing the insects, sweeping together into the sky as though to try their wings, swooping down towards the surface of the lake, then suspending themselves from the reeds which their weight scarcely bent, and filling them with their confused warbling.

Night would fall; the reeds stirred their fields of cat-tails and of rushes, and the whole feathered caravan, water-hens, teal, kingfishers, snipe, would fall silent; the lake surged upon its shores; the great voices of autumn spoke from the marshes and the woods: I drifted my boat ashore and returned to the château.

The section I have chosen for discussion and reproduced above comes to be dominated by birds, but it begins indirectly, with the statement that the sadness and isolation of autumn in the country are in keeping with the mood of the author. This is a necessary piece of information, though its relation to what follows is not as obvious as it may at first seem.

The second paragraph is a detour through the extended mechanical analogy between the characteristics of autumn and the fate of man. This systematically contrived discursus is artificial and irrelevant.[2] There is, indeed, a relation between autumn and human experience, but it does not show through Chateaubriand's grocery list ("this light that pales like our understanding, this sun that grows cold like our love," etc.) nor can it; the relation lies in the possibility of escaping the conceptual categories in which these very analogies have been made and transferring the activity of the mind to the objects of description.[3]

The question may be asked, "Why pursue this possibility of escaping conceptual categories?" Let us return to our birds.[4]

We may first observe that for all his "tristesse" in the autumn, Chateaubriand sees the return of the birds of passage with the autumn storms "with inexpressible pleasure." In his unhappiness, then, he must be finding happiness. The crows gather in large numbers on the flats near the pond, expressing a kind of assumption of authority by their multitudinous presence. When the dark judicial assembly have assumed their places at nightfall on the highest trees of the Mall, their dominance has been more fully asserted; we are awed by this new Parlement of Foules and await the instruction they reserve for themselves. The bluish haze at the forest crossroads and the lay of the wind signal a meaning which is that the world may be assumed by the self. In this sense Chateaubriand says "j'entrais en pleine possession des sympathies de ma nature," "I entered into full possession of the sympathies of my nature." This is the state in which true description may occur.

After a wasteful digression (added in a late version of the

manuscript and not reproduced above) on the *sylphide* that pursued his imagination, Chateaubriand comes back to real things—the birds again. No longer the crows, who established the tone; but the swallows who set in motion. What puts Chateaubriand in the state of mind that makes him willing and able to follow their swooping flight? It is the recognition of a quality in the birds that he knows to be the most important there is: to be without cause, to incarnate a principle of the non-conditioned and non-necessary; simply to be, and so to set the world in motion.

To be self-possessed puts one above nature. The swallows are neither earthbound nor even water-bound, their state is one of suspension in their own world. There is no discontinuity in their syntactic swoops, nothing divisible that would subject them to the measurements of this world. The succession of phrases, paratactic in effect, accumulating in a long series that is nevertheless the opposite of a periodic sentence, conveys the sense of the observer's commitment to the flowing sequences of external events rather than to the structure of his own logic. The observer is given over to an action taking place outside himself; and if the center and source of action lie in these outer things, they lie in the *self* of these outer things, and in one's own self as invested in that self.

Settling at last among the grasses of the pond, the swallows scarcely bend the reeds from which they suspend themselves; they remain apart; they do not interpenetrate with this world. The language they talk is just beyond the author's understanding, no matter how passionately he concentrates on their twittering code. The unseen crowd is in the reeds, but unseen, therefore not *of* the reeds. Unlike Yeats's birds and swans, who belong to both this world and another, Chateaubriand's belong to neither: strictly to their own. Their virtue, as I have said before, is their ability to be self-possessed and therefore perfect, in the sense (as I will try to show later) in which René wanted to be perfect. Yet their totally internal identity does not make them sterile, as Père Souël in his sermon at the end of *René* insists autism must make one; their inner life, independent of stimuli (to repeat), sets the world in motion.

The birds are the expression of a Self stirring in the world, deaf, blind, impervious, and supremely indifferent to the world and to all that does not seek to attach itself to It. But all efforts and pursuits other than that quest are either vain or harmful, being pursuits in the literal sense, forms of the search for purpose. Disaster is the one good fortune that may free one from the need for imposing an external motivation on oneself.

The career of René provides a good illustration of this problem: the destruction of motivation. Having sabotaged his practical life, René is still left with the necessity of protecting his radical subjectivity against the insistence of the outer world that he submit it to an external evaluation. Like Werther's, his tactic is withdrawal, though René does not commit suicide; he simply betakes himself, together with his inner self, to the forests of America. In a way René is a less advanced case of the Romantic schism between emotion and reason than either, say, Yorick, of Sterne's *Sentimental Journey*, or Werther. He himself has never reached the point of formulating his problem in terms of the conflict between faith in experience and intellectual doubt. René does not recognize any error at all in his own ways. He is no decadent Romantic, like Heine, consciously struggling against the rationalism in himself. The conflict does not take place between the two parts of a divided self, but rather between two kinds of ideal—Père Souël's rationalistic faith, in which conceptual order must prevail, and René's faith in his own subjectivity, for which both concepts and order are irrelevant.

Early in his life René had decided to commit suicide rather than go through the process of adapting to social norms. It is as though he had realized that the totality of satisfaction is not attainable by a compromise between inner and outer self, in "mature adjustment," and he will not accept life on such partial terms. As long as René has no excuse to exempt him from seeking a social role, he is desperately unhappy. Only after an irreparable calamity seems to put all possibility of adjustment out of the question can he breathe again. When he discovers that his sister has taken the veil because of an incestuous love for him, he is overjoyed, and there follows the notorious passage ending "Now that I was really unhappy I no longer felt any desire to die." He promptly departs for America to continue cultivating the vague treasure of his autistic self.

In the wilds of Louisiana, René, who has married an Indian girl but is not happy with her, is prevailed upon to divulge the secret of his morbid and solitary life to the missionary, Père Souël. The priest is not impressed by the solution René has found for his problems; he accuses him of nourishing a reciprocal incestuous love for his sister in an isolation propitious to smouldering passions. Furthermore, in concentrating his attention on himself and refusing to look outside, René is inventing a whole world of problems for himself, where none really exists: "all these troubles of which you complain are sheer nothingness." René's soul is shaped around a vortex of vacuities. Souël warns him that by isolating himself he is raising this self-concentration on emptiness to a dangerous pitch: "solitude . . . increases the powers of the soul while depriving them of all object." In the end, he who refuses to involve himself with his fellow-men will be punished by God: "sooner or later Heaven sends him a terrible punishment."

Père Souël's sermon may convince the reader, but it makes no visible impression on René. The end is a silent rejection of everything that Père Souël has argued. René vouchsafes no answer to the admonitions of his friends. He escapes the categories of Souël's sermon by his silence. He does not even articulate his rejection of the priest's advice, for the criteria Souël has applied to his behaviour are so remote from his understanding that no part of the sermon's meaning has impinged on him. So introverted is he that he does not even have to repudiate objectivity: he seems to be unconscious of the possibility that a standard of objectivity might exist.

But since René will not speak, a bird speaks for him. ". . . the voice of the flamingo could be heard, hidden in the reeds of the Mississippi, foretelling a storm in the middle of the day." A storm is expected at mid-day. Souël has warned René of heavenly retribution, but the storm cannot be taken as a portent that his prediction will be fulfilled. Père Souël has foreseen correctly that René's life will end catastrophically, but he does not understand the significance of the event which he predicts. The storm, and the tone of gloom with which the last page of *René* is imbrued, are if anything tokens of approbation rather than of punishment, a justification of René's way of life. The still small voice hidden in the reeds affirms the fitness of storm at mid-day and so reaffirms the reality of the stormy and the irrational in the midst of the sunlit world in which Souël has placed his trust. After all, Père Souël, for all his reason, dies by the same death as René, in the Indian massacre. As for René himself, he comes to the close of his life on his own terms.

> People say that, pressed by the two old men, he returned to his wife, but without finding happiness. He perished soon after with Chactas and Père Souël in the massacre of the French and the Natchez in Louisiana. The rock where he used to sit at sunset is still pointed out.

René, by his refusal to respond to Père Souël's meaning, or rather by making the reader feel that there is nothing to respond to, has achieved a reversal of values, as Meursault does by rejecting the false values of *his* priest at the end of

L'Etranger. After the sermon, we begin to realize that what had seemed pure "néant" to Souël is to René the "matière" and the "réel." It is Souël's rationalism, or, more precisely, his abstractionism, hiding under the guise of practicality, that is the "néant." Not Souël's practical peace, but René's impractical storm, as I have said, is the norm of the worthwhile life. The life which orients itself by abstract categories and which functions through conscious decisions loses its opportunity for the discovery of its kernel of independence. That independence, which it would have shared with the world, is recognized by an affinity with realities rather than by concentrated attention to the "cogito" and its structures.

There is an intentionality detached from us, which description is an attempt to reach. But René, saint of subjectivity, seems to seek something more. Avoiding the mimesis of the transcendent selfhood that resides in reality, he seems to move directly towards an attempt to express it in his own being. In his total solipsism, unconditioned and detached from anything which could move him, he becomes the embodiment of an unmodified, unqualified identity.

One might object that all this is to take Chateaubriand too seriously; that at best he is an irresponsible writer, at worst a liar and a hypocrite, but never someone whose words should be counted and weighed for their depth of meaning. It may be acknowledged, broadly speaking, that Chateaubriand is a hypocrite, but his achievements would be impossible without his hypocrisy. The total absorption in things of which he is capable is not in keeping with a conscious, logical mind; it is not possible to accept without reserve the standards of a phenomenally dominant world at one time, and to withdraw to a detached and measured appraisal of that same world at the next moment. The return to the realm of objectivity takes place, but in blatant bad faith; Chateaubriand will play games in that field, but he will never take it seriously. To be truthful in a milieu of categories is to capitulate to the first law of abstraction. Chateaubriand's unhesitating hypocrisy is simply the other side of the coin of description. If there were a middle ground, the boundary of the description would be less clear, the absolute emergence of the description would be compromised. When one returns from submersion in reality, one does not return to lucidity, but simply to non-being. It is noteworthy how fast the egotist Chateaubriand gets himself out of the way once he goes out on the pond in his boat. He moves himself there, then brushes himself aside; he is not eager to parade his pseudo-identity when his true identity, vested in outer things, can come into play. Chateaubriand's is an ego that never lets itself be caught in the light of day, never allows itself to be honestly appraised or seeks to appraise itself objectively, because its destiny is within nature, not outside it in a conscious, separate self. Chateaubriand prefers hypocrisy to a self-consciousness which is self-betrayal.

In the end we are compensated for the artificiality of Chateaubriand's poses in the non-phenomenal world. When one enters his descriptions, one *is* the lake beating on its shores, one is within and is it. There is a sense of darkness that rises from each of his descriptions at the point at which it turns real, which is the point at which the "I" has become "it." It is not a pompous proclamation, "make me thy lyre," or "I am like the forest," but the forest has simply sponged up my sense of identity and I am in it as itself. Camus, on the other hand, feels not only a "présence au monde;" he feels at once "mon détachement de moi-même et ma présence au monde" ("my detachment from myself and my presence in the world"—*Noces*, p. 33). For Chateaubriand the first term is lacking. Camus, like Chateaubriand, plunges into the object, but unlike Chateaubriand, he does not lose himself in it. He is still painfully conscious of his being there in it, imprisoned in it and as it were glumly looking out, like the student Anselmus from his bottle in Hoffmann's "The Golden Pot."

There is a peculiar force in the true descriptive style which takes over when one surrenders self in favour of the object; it is the force of an unbroken continuity. Verb forms, instead of coming to an end, as transitive action, directed from the agent at the world, comes to an end, participate instead in a continuum in which every action is reflexive, intermediate between passive and active. The actions, or "verbs," have no objects. In a line of John Gibson Lockhart's, describing the west coast of Scotland, the hills receding in interminable succession, he says, looked

> on the remoter wastes of water over which their eternal shadows lay brooding and blackening into deeper and wider gloom, as the last crimson line of sunset kept sinking down lower and lower in the western horizon. *Adam Blair* (Edinburgh, 1963), p. 153.

The shadows "blacken;" but they do not blacken something, they do not merely get more black, they "blacken" in some kind of in-between dimension of action. It is the same with "Elles se jouaient sur l'eau" or "les roseaux agitaient leurs champs de quenouilles et de glaives;" there is a perpetual recurrence to reflexive or semi-reflexive forms, "se venaient suspendre," "se rabattaient," or in *Les Natchez* before the storm, "La nature se voile; les paysages s'agrandissent;" etc.[5]

A dominant feature of the descriptive style, then (in spite of what Lessing says in *Laokoön*), is continuity. When we act, or when we think about the world from a detached position, we create discontinuity; engagement in the self of the external world annuls the discreteness of action and continuity becomes possible. The law of the mind, from thought to thought and from thought to observation, is discontinuity; the law of description is the absence of the discontinuous. Description is a triumph over the observer. It erases the hiatuses of the observer's perception even though when incorporated in language it must name the objects of perception in series. For all its appearance of parataxis, the sentence on the swallows does not release us for an instant from their actions. These actions are not merely our limited, deliberate actions; they have the sweep and the intensity of things that happen without our having had to engender them; all our energy can go into the experience, none has to be spent on generating, defining, or organizing it. As we follow the birds, or move with the lake, we discover a sense of action, not mere occasions in nature. These actions become one's own actions and "one's own actions" can cease to occur.[6] Speaking of losing the self when absorbed in landscape, Coleridge says: "Ghost of a mountain—the forms seizing my Body as I passed & became realities—I, a Ghost, till I had reconquered my Substance."[7]

The self plunges into events and finds its organization in them. But at this point an insoluble problem arises. How can one speak of the organization of events which one is no longer viewing, and which by definition have no more organization than nature has laws? "Il y a des lieux où meurt l'esprit pour que naisse la vérité qui est sa négation même." ("There are places where the mind dies so that the truth which is its very negation may be born." Camus, *Essais* [Paris, 1965], p. 1350.) "Plongée dans la beauté, l'intelligence fait son repas de néant." ("When it plunges into beauty, the understanding feeds on nothingness," Camus, *Noces*, p. 93.) In fact, "Devant ces paysages . . . chacune de ses pensées [de l'intelligence] est une rature sur l'homme." ("In the face of such scenes . . . each thought is a blot on man." *Noces*, p. 34.) How can a purely phenomenal field have organization, and how can we even think of describing its organization if it does have one? ". . . il [l'homme] n'est plus rien devant le monde que cette tache informe qui ne connaît de vérité que passive." (". . . man then becomes nothing more before the world than this shapeless blot that knows only a passive truth." *Noces*, p. 93). Nevertheless we experience the scene in Chateaubriand as something that organizes us, and not merely in the categories of sequence or of spatial direction. The nature of this organization I find impossible to articulate. A simple allegorical reading—to say, for instance, that in this passage we move from activity to peace (or at least suspension) [8]—such a reading is a conceptual reduction of the scene, an interpretation, and as such it lacks the special quality of an exteriorization, in which the details are the truth. As St.-Jean Perse would say, "[les oiseaux] ne remontent point le cours d'une abstraction." ("[the birds] do not follow an abstraction upstream.") "Tache frappée comme d'un sceau, elle n'est pourtant chiffre ni sceau, n'étant signe ni symbole, mais la chose même dans son fait et sa fatalité." ("Mark stamped as by a seal, it is nevertheless neither cipher nor seal, being neither sign nor symbol, but the thing itself in its facticity and its fatality." *Oiseaux* [Paris, 1963], p. 31, p. 13). And a geometrical account of the passage, as of composition in a drawing, would tell us even less about the whole experience.

In narrative, in plot, in dialogue, one can see the control of a conceptual scheme at work: but encountering a passage of pure description in the midst of a self-explicating genre, whether it be novel or journal, one has no source of terms with which to describe the description. The blank refusal of nature to organize itself, to move into our capacity for focus a set of intelligible coordinates, makes the planned treatment of a descriptive passage uncommonly difficult. Though nature is benevolent, one might almost grow frightened at this confrontation with a body that will not tell its shape, and sense beneath some hidden giant who refuses to show his lineaments, and who might best not be disturbed, a kind of Leviathan or Moby-Dick. Two curious passages from

Gogol come to mind in this connection: one refers to a portrait with frightening eyes:

> After all, it is only a picture, painted from a model. Then why on earth should it give me this strangely unpleasant feeling? Or is a faithful, slavish imitation of nature already an offence and must affect you like a loud, discordant scream? Or if you approach your subject objectively and coolly, without feeling any particular sympathy for it, must it necessarily confront you in all its singular terrible reality, unillumined by the light of any unfathomable thought hidden in everything? [9]

As Robbe-Grillet says of Kafka's descriptions (and it could be said with equal truth of the landscapes of a contemporary of Gogol's such as Captain Michael Scott, whose style is strongly reminiscent of Robbe-Grillet's),[10] "L'effet d'hallucination provient de leur netteté extraordinaire . . . Rien n'est plus fantastique, en définitive, que la précision." ("The effect of hallucination comes from their extraordinary clarity . . . Nothing is finally more fantastic than exactness." *Pour un nouveau roman* [Paris, 1963], p. 180).

The second passage from Gogol comes at the end of one of his ghost stories, "The Terrible Vengeance," where the last and worst of a long line of malefactors meets his end:

> . . . all the dead men leapt into the abyss, seized the dead man as he was falling and fastened their teeth into him. Another, taller and more terrible than the rest, tried to rise from the ground, but he could not, for he had not the strength to do it, so huge had he grown in the earth; and if he had risen out of the earth he would have overturned the Carpathian mountains, the whole of the Semigrad and the Turkish lands. (*Tales of Good and Evil*, pp. 56–57).

As I have said, I see no solution to this problem: what principle of order can emerge from a phenomenal field in which the viewer is submerged? Even if concepts and linguistic patterns may once have entered into the constitution of a perception, they cannot be regarded as governing the phenomenal field at the time when one is actually immersed in the perception.[11]

The search for an organizing principle in landscape is finally self-annihilating and may even lead to the sense that the search for a similar principle in art in general, even in a genre that is apparently controlled by concepts, such as the novel, is wrong. Eventually, one may also come to feel that the whole notion that a conceptual organizing principle is the crucial thing in the work of art is false. A concept gives us a foothold in a work, a kind of stepping-stone in the stream, but there are no more stepping-stones beyond and one cannot cross.[12]

The most I can hope for in dealing with this perplexing problem is the bare hint of an answer: that for the artist the difficulty may not be so serious. The forms of the mental world and of the physical world are for him the same forms because the worlds are the same worlds, "Un même espace poétique" ("The same poetic space"—St.-Jean Perse, *Oiseaux*, p. 14). In this sense a description is no different from a fantasy. To probe another horizon: perhaps for the artist the forms are his needs. As Rousseau or Schopenhauer would say, desire, not theory, is the parent of concepts; and it may be that for all of us categories are born at the discretion of our needs, coming as an after-thought to articulate or limb them out. Categories are not a basic category. Perhaps concepts merely provide the raw material for metaphors. They are instrumental rather than constitutive, and reality is put together for convenience out of what we decide to know only for the sake of what we want. Art is a state of desire, not of "phenomenal field" at all; or, to put it differently, it is a state of what we want, therefore we do not have to know. The question then becomes (if we are still assuming that an organizational principle must be found), what is the organization of the field of pure desire, rather than what is the organization of the field of phenomena. But there again I am left, though less anxious, still without an answer.

The problem of the constitution of the phenomenal field is not as important for Rousseau as it is for Chateaubriand. In Rousseau, the objects of description fade out instead of solidifying as a goal. To me it seems that both authors have missed something, and that (to allow myself an aside in the transition from Chateaubriand to Rousseau) by accepting as extremes perception and non-perception they lose the awareness of an alternative that includes both the others. There is no need either to seek or to avoid percepts. The ideal perception of nature is neither an acute consciousness of its details nor an immersion in reverie that makes all consciousness fade out. The second is deficient because it becomes (avowedly) an absorption with self rather than with nature; the first is inadequate because it makes a stab at contact with nature which must be renewed repeatedly to keep the experience alive. This is essentially an outsider's view of landscape, the visitor's view; or perhaps, for Chateaubriand, the remembered view of something that had been a more pervasive kind of experience in his childhood. In this sense the detail-less, swimming emotionality of atmosphere in *René* has a certain advantage over the retrospective precision of the *Mémoires d'outre-tombe.* Of course, one cannot remember the experience and be immersed in it at the same time, Wordsworth to the contrary notwithstanding, and relatively speaking Chateaubriand achieves a great deal with the method of the *Mémoires.* But his feeling does not go past the initial stage of noticing a landscape, to the point of being embedded in the awareness of the surroundings, unconscious, not looking. Nature is not something one must look at, then achieve an experience of; the situation of looking at something (cf. Bashō) should never arise if contact with nature has really been achieved; the whole thing should be acting continuously, not in parts or as repeated discrete experiences. It is all there in advance. It is a luxury and a sensuous satisfaction, surrounding, imbuing one, so that one can sit and write (as I do now) without any loss of the experience and one can look up at the mountains without any great gain of it. It is being hammocked in the surroundings, not making a gesture towards them.

A blindness is the essence, not a seeing; a change in the matrix of vision and feeling, in which acts have a different quality. It is not that by some act one achieves a moment of vision. It is the whole state that *is* vision (i.e. every act is a seeing).

Of this attitude there seems to be more in Rousseau than in Chateaubriand, though it is not exactly what I have been describing, since in Rousseau the ideal perception leads to an abandonment of awareness. At least in Rousseau, one does look through rather than at the phenomenal field, existing at its level like the leaves of the water-lily at the level of the pond, so that one is finally looking in or with it rather than at it. Like Chateaubriand, Rousseau takes to his boat, but eventually in order to escape percepts rather than to intensify or enrich his field of vision (*Oeuvres complètes,* I, 1044).

> J'allais me jeter seul dans un bateau que je conduisais au milieu du lac quand l'eau était calme, et là, m'étendant tout de mon long dans le bateau les yeux tournés vers le ciel, je me laissais aller et dériver lentement au gré de l'eau, quelquefois pendant plusieurs heures, plongé dans mille rêveries confuses mais délicieuses, et qui sans avoir aucun objet bien déterminé ni constant ne laissaient pas d'être

à mon gré cent fois préférables à tout ce que j'avais trouvé
de plus doux dans ce qu'on appelle les plaisirs de la vie.

I would throw myself into a boat and go out alone into the
middle of the lake when the water was calm, and there,
stretched out at full length in the boat looking up at the
sky, I would let myself go and drift slowly at the will of the
water, sometimes for many hours, plunged in a thousand
confused but delicious reveries, which without having any
clearly determined or constant object were nonetheless to
my taste a hundred times better than anything I had found
sweetest in what people call the pleasures of life.

There may be a momentary temptation to draw an analogy between the solipsism of René and Rousseau's withdrawal from contact with his surroundings, but the similarity
is deceptive. There is something hard and closed in René's
silence which is quite unlike the expansive ecstasy with
which Rousseau's self melts into the substratum of Being.
It is as though René had swallowed the key to the secret of
the world; Rousseau is himself that key. But I cannot hope
to present Rousseau's descriptive style more successfully than
Jean Starobinski has done in *Jean-Jacques Rousseau: La
transparence et l'obstacle*.[13] The movement of revelation of
the truth behind appearances in Rousseau is not the revelation of a truth in things, or of a true-thing, but of the self.
"He can give up the intention of achieving an objective
revelation of nature, because presence-to-the-self is accompanied by a feeling of expansion in which, without asking
anything of *things* and without really confronting the world,
the ecstasy of his inner transparency is transformed into an
ecstasy of the Whole. . . . the 'mystic' experience of Being
makes the material unveiling of nature superfluous. To un-
veil is still an action. . . . Now Rousseau achieves a joy of
Being that transcends all active knowing: what he experi-

ences deliciously is the *immediate* presence of Being itself
unveiling itself." "Without going out of itself, and in the
swoon of a Dionysiac intoxication, consciousness possesses
itself (and loses itself) as absolute immediacy with respect to
both itself and all other things." "Nature is no longer an
external spectacle to be unveiled, it becomes totally present
to the 'inner sense.'" "To be oneself and see reality: he
wants to achieve both one and the other, one at the same
time as the other."

The purity of vision achieved by becoming totally self
is attested by the hostility of others who demand a commitment to truth located in objects and who cannot permit
Rousseau's expressed contempt for their raison d'être to go
unchallenged. Oddly, yet inevitably, raison d'être and epis-
temology turn out to be the same thing, and not only for
Rousseau and his persecutors, but also for their mirror-
image, Meursault and his judges in *L'Etranger*. Instead of
achieving innocence by becoming totally Self, Meursault
achieves it by a denial of subjectivity or of the existence of
self as such (quite a Sartrean and also a Humean position).
Rousseau and Meursault are condemned for opposite reasons: Rousseau for being totally Self and for not being the
Other, for refusing to adopt the standpoint of the Other
(i.e. of objects); Meursault, for not being the fictitious,
factitious subjective self filled into the lacunae of the self-
as-objects by a theory of self which is a lie. Meursault can
appreciate vision fully—(Camus—"At Tipasa, 'I see' is the
equivalent of 'I believe'")[14]—because his only self resides
in what he sees. He is purged of pseudo-self. One (Rousseau)
seeks transparency, the other only the opaque.[15]

Yet Rousseau and Camus share one attitude towards the
role of landscape, and this distinguishes them sharply from
Chateaubriand. For neither is the beauty of landscape important in itself. Rousseau is as indifferent to the mere

beauty of the world's *scene* as Meursault himself—he is responsive only to the world's meaning or to its relationship with him. This is the meaning of the generality, what one might call the "classical" descriptive style, in some of Rousseau's deliberate landscape-drawings: "scene" or description is a shallower view of the world, as decorative, and is not to be taken seriously; [16] a scene is like a stage-setting, independent, less related to the action than is the Rousseau or the Meursault world. Phenomenologically it expresses the naïve assumption that the world is independent of the mind or viewer. Meursault and Rousseau never let go of the world as the field of experience only, never seriously set out to describe it "for its own sake." [17] Rousseau describes objects only in order eventually to withdraw from them; he dwells on a landscape to bring the self, not the landscape, into focus. Finally the world can be known only in absentia. Contrarily, in Camus one does not have the pathetic fallacy which all description of the beauties of nature, no matter how convincing, must be; one has the *indifference* of the world which one feels when one identifies it as the field of experience, and *it* makes the description. ". . . je m'ouvrais pour la première fois à la *tendre indifférence* du monde. De l'éprouver si pareil à moi, si fraternel enfin, j'ai senti que j'avais été heureux, et que je l'étais encore." (Italics mine). It is a "tender" indifference only because the objects and the world are oneself, therefore tender towards oneself or expressive of concern for the self ("fraternel"); yet they are indifferent because they are object not subject. The world expresses us. That relationship it has to us therefore is tender. But that is all the tenderness it has.

In Rousseau, as I have said, there are two landscape worlds; one the classical vague or empty one, from which he really turns away. Perhaps this is "society's" landscape, a property of what Starobinski calls "L'universel humain" in which Rousseau does not participate. The other is the immediate closed world of the sense experiences that express L'Etre (Being). Meursault perhaps has two also.[18] The first is sea and sun, the intense but vague or directionless preconscious experience of the young, animated by "that physical fear of the animal that loves the sun." (*Noces*, p. 36). In that phase, even the coming of birds at nightfall can teach him nothing, he ignores the need to understand; they remain merely background: "Maintenant, les arbres s'étaient peuplés d'oiseaux. La terre soupirait lentement avant d'entrer dans l'ombre. Tout à l'heure, avec la première étoile, la nuit tombera sur la *scène* du monde. . . ." ("Now, the trees had peopled themselves with birds. The earth breathed slowly before sinking into darkness. Soon, with the first star, night will fall on the *scene* of the world. . . ." *Noces*, p. 17. Italics mine). It takes death to convert the background-vision of *Noces* into the intimate vision of *L'Etranger*. Beyond that stage, like the voyager of the *Divine Comedy* emerging from Hell, Meursault emerges into consciousness in the starry night of the prison, a night which is no longer background but reality itself.

In neither Rousseau nor Camus, however, can landscape stand alone as it does in Chateaubriand, who occupies a position both above and below Rousseau and Camus in his conception of nature. He too has his vague conventional settings, which do not record any lived experience,[19] and his intensely engaging reality, when the birds have arrived. But the cleavage comes in a different part of the spectrum. When Chateaubriand puts his full potential into landscape description as such, he is not merely providing background. He ends, as it were, before the point at which they begin. Chateaubriand's true descriptions carry the full force of his unqualified consciousness; they do not melt into the self like Rousseau's, nor do they like Camus' turn the space between self and non-self into a tympanum of pain.[20]

Simplistic in their approach to experience, they restore our confidence in vision; indifferent to dialectic, they begin to reapproach the naïve poetry of Schiller's definition in "Über Naïve und Sentimentalische Dichtung" and the demonstrative art of Hegel's "symbolic" or primitive periods. They confirm our sense, for which Rousseau and Camus only strive, that the outer world and the inner world are "un même espace poétique," are one.

❧ 4 ❧

An End to Innocence

Innocence may be compared to a luxuriant weed.
GÜNTER GRASS

IT WAS AT A TIME when innocence was being praised and
illustrated by such writers as Blake, Rousseau, and Wordsworth that Friedrich Schiller articulated the dilemma of innocence so sharply as to make it appear insoluble for artist
and philosopher alike. There are two kinds of poetry, he
said, in the "Essay on Simple and Sentimental Poetry": the
simple and the sentimental. Simple poetry is innocent;
sentimental poetry tries to be innocent. Unfortunately, to
try to be innocent is a contradiction in terms. The harder
one tries, the less possibility there is of succeeding, for the
effort itself is a component of the deficiency, is itself the
sin, so to speak, and the consciousness which informs us that
we have lost our innocence is also the cause of our loss of
innocence. The Greeks possessed innocence, says Schiller,
but modern man no longer does. "They experienced things
naturally; we [merely] experience the Natural." [1] Nature
and the natural vanish from the subject and reappear as an
idea, or object, of literature. Once man has achieved a

developed culture, there is an end of inner harmony; he can no longer express himself as a unity, but only as a being who pursues unity. The naïve or innocent poetry of primitive mankind can be a representation of reality, but the sentimental poetry of modern man must be the representation of an ideal, that is, of something acknowledged to be unreal. The idyll, the elegy, or the satire are our only remaining vehicles of expression. The idyll describes an imaginary reality, the elegy laments a lost reality, and the satire does not so much express reality as it rejects it.

Man's inability to find repose, his restless oscillation between the position of subject and of object in his search for an eternally elusive unity, is a major concern of Diderot, of Fichte, of Hegel, as well as of Schiller. Diderot in *Rameau's Nephew* presents the type of man who has entered into Hegel's so-called "phase of Culture." [2] The Nephew, by his very identification as a nephew, is not himself. He is just someone's nephew, and he knows himself as a partial but unsatisfactory reflection of his famous uncle. Yet he cannot be his uncle, either. In his own life his identity is determined by the wealthy families it is his profession to entertain. He *is* whatever they want him to be. If for an instant he tries to assert some independent identity he is lost—quite literally: he loses his job. As toady, sycophant, parasite, he must relinquish all claims to an authentic self. His life, like that of most people, consists of pantomime, and what he is remains eternally in doubt.

But the pursuit of a social identity that obscures one's inner identity is not the real problem, although it has been the subject of incessant complaint from Rousseau to Heidegger. The real problem is that consciousness itself, without the intervention of other people, produces a division between the inner and outer dimensions of the self. In achieving consciousness, the mind moves to an objective plane outside the self, from which it can contemplate both the self and the external world as external to itself. Yet there is a contradiction involved in this development; for this external self, or platform-self, is after all just an agency or dimension of the self, and to the extent that it acquires an objective or independent existence it is false and unnatural, a synthetic product which denies the very principle of selfhood or subjectivity. A self which has become an object is a contradiction in terms. The attempt of the self to escape the status of an object is the pursuit of innocence, the attempt to recapture the primal, pre-conscious harmony. But it is an attempt which is doomed, for the self that wishes to recall its object-self, to withdraw the limb which it had extruded, so to speak, is already compromised. It has been guilty of the original act of objectification; it is contaminated with self-consciousness. And consciousness is incompatible with innocence; inevitably, it leads towards experience, a sinister state which in these terms turns out to be strangely similar to abstraction or theory. It is no accident that the hero of *Peter Schlemihl* is forced to become a scientist once he has forfeited his natural relationships with other people by selling his shadow to the devil. Of course, knowledge from the Garden of Eden on has been indissolubly linked with experience and with sin. Knowledge detached from human need is the basic guilt: and a world objectified in terms of such knowledge is the world of experience, or the modern Hell, as Blake would put it.

So far, the period under consideration seems to show as much awareness of the loss of innocence as conviction of its actual or impending return. In fact, every period has had similar concerns. Innocence was not some new fad of the "romantic revival." From the Old Testament, through the Pelagian heresy of the fifth century, to the moral optimism of Shaftesbury, the problem comes into focus again and again. Along the way there is the pastoral tradition, from Theocritus, through Dio Chrysostom, to Sidney, Montaigne, and the cult of the noble savage. The major poem of seventeenth-century England, *Paradise Lost,* deals with the loss of innocence; the greatest German seventeenth-century novel is entitled *Simplicissimus;* the pursuit of the primitive in every form throughout the eighteenth century is a forlorn hope for the recovery of innocence. But the simultaneous lament about the decline of poetry (there are exceptions, such as Young's *Conjectures,* but they are rare) betrays the conviction that civilization is fatal to man's emotional powers. On all sides we hear that the growth of knowledge spells the death of the imagination. Shakespeare could be great only because he was *not* learned. The apparent defeat of the spontaneous and creative by the reflective and abstract leads to two incompatible solutions: Rousseau's suggestion that we return to the woods,[3] and Peacock's advice (in "The Four Ages of Poetry") that we dispense with poetry altogether, since the poetic principle is dead in any case.

During the period of our inquiry, which begins with the late eighteenth century, there are a number of works explicitly concerned with innocence. We could enter the subject through Bernardin de St. Pierre's *Paul et Virginie,* through Burns, or through Blake; we could approach it through that strange but engaging medical work, Gotthilf Heinrich von Schubert's *Die Symbolik des Traumes* (Bamberg, 1814), which contains one of the most appealing and reasonable pleas in literature for the restoration of our unity of consciousness (pp. 159 ff.); but I prefer to take Friedrich de la Motte-Fouqué's *Undine* as my principal example.[4] Although, like some of my other instances, it may be regarded as intrinsically slight, it may also, like the others, be seen as paradigmatic; for instance, it prefigures the pattern of the relation between the sexes which is usually associated with Dostoyevsky. It is a difficult book to talk about, for the explicitness of its idealism and its unpretentious yet unashamed sweetness do not really demand a hearing in a world dominated by the heavy-handed metaphysical brutality of the Kierkegaard tradition. Undine has not really survived, though many wish she had, as we can see in the attempts of Hans Christian Andersen and Jean Giraudoux to revive her. Undine should, properly, be left alone. However, since the book comes as close to realizing innocence in one of its major forms as any work of the period, we have a commitment to speak of it, if also a commitment not to do it too harsh injustice by reducing it to an illustration in a philosophy of history.

The story begins with the arrival of a young knight at the shore of a lake which lies beyond an enchanted forest he has just traversed. On a peninsula jutting out into the lake lives an old fisherman with his wife. They receive their visitor, Huldbrand, with genuine pleasure and true hospitality, but their greeting is interrupted by the arrival of a quicksilvery, wilful, temperamental girl, totally spoiled and uncontrollable, who appears to be their daughter. On being crossed in a whim, she stamps out into the night, and we learn from her foster-father's account that the girl, Undine, is really a changeling, who had appeared at his door after his own child had disappeared into the lake.

The knight, Huldbrand, and the old fisherman set out in pursuit of the errant Undine, and Huldbrand discovers her on an island in the midst of a torrent that is about to cut off the peninsula from the mainland with its swelling waters. Huldbrand wades out to the island where Undine is lying in the moonlight, apparently completely unafraid, and not in the least inclined to rejoin her family. In fact, she wants to keep Huldbrand with her on the island for the night. When she finally agrees to return, she does so only at the instance of the knight, not because of any sense of impropriety in her behaviour or of duty or guilt towards her foster-parents. The one feeling of which Undine is incapable is guilt. *She is innocent.*

The innocence of Undine at the beginning of this story is identified with instinct. She is innocent because she possesses complete instinctual freedom. She does not know the meaning of repression or voluntary self-frustration. When Huldbrand tells her that he undertook his journey through the perils of the enchanted forest at the instigation of a beautiful lady by the name of Bertalda, Undine doesn't brood or nurse her jealousy: she simply bites him on the finger. There is not a trace of masochism about her. This absence of self-restraint, which seems quite compatible with bursts of impetuous love, marks her behaviour until her marriage.

For Huldbrand does marry her, almost perforce. The peninsula has been sundered from the mainland by the torrent and has become an island. The two young people are caught in a necessary intimacy which neither of them seems to abhor, and when a priest is driven by a storm to the shores of the island Huldbrand asks him to marry them. Meanwhile Undine's behaviour grows inexplicably wilder and more freakish until the very night of the ceremony; but the next morning she is completely transformed.

The reason for this metamorphosis we learn soon after. Undine was, indeed, an undine—one of Paracelsus' water-spirits; a mermaid, daughter of a powerful king in the Mediterranean Sea. But as a mermaid, she has no soul; totally moved by the elements and the natural forces of the world, she will, at the end of her life, dissolve and return to them. Her father wants her to acquire a soul, and with it, immortality; but in order to achieve this she must love and be loved by a human being. On the night of her marriage she was still without a soul; but in the morning she awoke with one.

It becomes immediately clear that the acquisition of a
soul is a mixed blessing, and Undine's anxieties about her
transformation are rapidly justified. Gone is her whimsicality, gone her puckish impulsiveness; she is now all conscience and tender heart, as Chaucer would say. The perfection of her former freedom is wrought into the totality
of love. But with the experience of love comes the capacity
for sorrow; the other face of mature love is pain. Still,
Undine proves equal to the occasion. Founded on her total
instinctual freedom, her humanity is likewise without flaw;
the incapacity for falsehood or for guilt that had been her
birthright as a force of nature is transmitted intact to her
adult phase. Undine has remained innocent or, better still,
through the act of love she has achieved a higher form of
innocence that transcends the mechanical innocence of
childhood.

The testing of Undine's soul begins all too soon. Huldbrand returns to the city, where Bertalda quickly attaches
herself to him again. Undine, now as incapable of expressing
jealousy as she had formerly been incapable of suppressing
it, shows Bertalda every sign of love and kindness and in-
voluntarily encourages a triangular relationship to develop.
In the meanwhile, Huldbrand has been growing more and
more uneasy with his too-perfect wife and feels his kinship
increasing with the less ideal and therefore more human
Bertalda. It is as though too much soul were even less appropriate for a human being than too little; and poor
Undine once more must suffer for her perfection. Her
achieved humanity is even less viable among mankind than
her instinctual nature had been. Innocence has no place
among us, and Undine is driven back into the water to join
the spirits of her kind.

Long before this point in the story, it has become obvious
that it was not Undine who had borrowed a soul from
Huldbrand, but Huldbrand who was dependent on her for

as much soul as he could muster. By the end of the story their roles have been completely reversed. What little he has learned from Undine Huldbrand is about to forfeit. By marrying Bertalda, by rejecting the very memory of Undine, he will be lost, and, quite literally, damned, for Undine alone had introduced a troth into his life. If he drives out her memory, he loses his only feeble claim to humanity. Undine must save him from himself, and she does: she saves his soul. Rising from the well, which Bertalda had unstopped to get water for her vain ablutions, Undine comes to Huldbrand on the eve of his wedding, and embraces him, weeping, until he dies.

Innocence has had its revenge. Although we may not be able to live with it, we certainly cannot live without it. Unrealizable ideal though it may be, fiction, fancy, fairy-tale, it has enough reality to be a matter of life and death: perhaps, *the* matter; for, as we see in Huldbrand's case, even life without Undine in some form is merely a living death. The fact that innocence has no place on earth does not absolve us of the obligation to keep faith with it.

Throughout *Undine,* the fact that innocence is rooted in instinct is constantly emphasized. It is no saintly abstraction; it wells from our desires. As Diderot had said, "Innocence, as I understand it, can be found in violent passions as well as in tranquil emotions." [5] Even after she assumes a soul, Undine is in continuous contact with the submarine sources of her power. Her uncle, the water prince Kühleborn, is constantly threatening Huldbrand, constantly raging to destroy Bertalda, and it is only by sleepless vigilance that Undine can quell his rebellion, i.e. the rebellion of her instinctual self. She apologizes to Huldbrand for Kühleborn's inability to take her rejection lightly: it is because, she says, his poor nature, a mere elemental mirror of the external world, cannot understand that sorrow and joy are one in love: "He doesn't believe a word I say," she laments.

When Undine, Bertalda, and Huldbrand go boating on the
Danube, the water positively writhes with teeming protest,
the goblins of instinct can no longer contain themselves. The
well on the castle grounds is a standing threat to the precarious order above. Finally, Undine does, after all, return
to the element from which she had sprung, and in the end
it is the protest of the water that washes away Huldbrand's
besmirched life in a baptism of tears. Still, these tears are
water, and water in this story is instinctual truth. From
instinct comes innocence, then: as Jakob Boehme had said
several centuries earlier, "We all in the Originality of our
Life have the Source of the Anger, and of the Fierceness, or
else we should not be alive; but we must look to it, and in
ourselves go forth out of the Source of that Fierceness with
God, and generate the Love in us." [6]

The road from Boehme through La Motte-Fouqué to
D. H. Lawrence and Herbert Marcuse's *Eros and Civilization* lies clear before us. Throughout, innocence must be
reached, as Blake puts it, through an improvement in sensuous delight, until the whole body becomes an erogenous
zone. More generally speaking, innocence, so far considered,
is the ability to feel.

As the ability to feel, it must once more be contrasted
with its apparent inhibitor, the ability to think. *Faust* (Part
I), another major work of the period under consideration,
documents the triumph of thought over sympathy. The
"wicked whisper" of doubt that prevented the Ancient
Mariner from praying is heard at Faust's ear when he is
contemplating the betrayal of Gretchen. In Charles Maturin's Gothic novel, *Melmoth the Wanderer,* one section is
devoted to the story of Immalee, a young girl who has been
abandoned in childhood on an idyllic island in the Indian
Ocean and has grown up there alone. She is visited by Melmoth, who exhibits to her the nature of the world beyond
the island. Her reaction is summed up in one sentence:

"The world that thinks does not feel." [7] Like Eve, she too is tempted to think; like Undine, she learns that in thought lies suffering. With Manfred she might say, "The tree of knowledge is not that of Life." It is interesting that that modern champion of innocence, Jean Giraudoux, should have taken a story similar to Immalee's for the subject of one of his novels, *Susanne et le Pacifique,* and even more interesting that the whole theme of children's shipwreck should have been so devastatingly inverted by William Golding in *Lord of the Flies.* In case the point was not yet clear, Golding wrote a still more obvious "end to innocence" in *The Inheritors.*

The loss of feeling, then, is the loss of innocence; but here we are confronted with a problem of sequence. Is it the intrusion of abstract reason, dragging behind it its inescapable poor relation, the so-called material world, that drives out emotion? Or is it the loss of feeling that lets in reason and the material world, that permits them to assert their supremacy over our lives? In *Undine,* the answer is categorical: it must be the latter, for the simple reason that no conflict with the external or material world is ever envisaged in the book. Environment does not impinge on the lovers to make them unhappy; a materialistic interpretation of experience is never allowed to cast a dubious light on the ideal. The ideal fails for Huldbrand not because of any external pressure but because of his own inner insufficiency: a kind of inadequacy that some may call original sin.

I shall turn now from the positive versions of innocence, which have given us some of the most appealing works of modern literature (I think of the lyrics of Burns, of Grillparzer's *Der arme Spielmann,* of *Huckleberry Finn,* of *Billy Budd,* of Wilde's fairy-tales, of Rilke's *Geschichten vom lieben Gott,* of St. Exupéry's *Le Petit Prince*), to some of the other forms assumed by this idea. There is a whole group of manifestations of the innocence principle that does not fit into any of the familiar areas of the subject. These may be referred to as the experiential forms of innocence or the negative versions of innocence: innocence approached through another channel and not directly exhibited as such. In fact, the example with which I intend to start, the thought of the Marquis de Sade, is not usually recognized as pertaining to a cult of innocence by any definition. Nevertheless, this author provides, for me, a crucial illustration.

De Sade does not begin with the naïve assumption that our innocence is waiting in the wings, ready to come out and embrace us at a cue. On the contrary; innocence is known by its absence and must be apprehended through its absence. There is no innocence in positive form left in us, and all discoveries or rediscoveries of a positive innocence are mere hypocrisy. Innocence must be refashioned from the only material we have available to us in our totally corrupt condition; innocence has taken refuge in sin, and must be rediscovered in sin. Emotion, when it has died as love, may be resurrected as hate. Cruelty, if genuinely enjoyed and not hopelessly vitiated by self-consciousness, may contain more authentic feeling than apparent kindness. It may also contain more individuality than a collective ethic which is not experienced as real by any individual. It is not only positive innocence that is at loggerheads with society; negative innocence has just as little possibility of reaching a compact with collectivity. The law is its bugbear, not because law will punish it—on the contrary: law is the right arm of organized crime. But law is abstract, its punishments do not derive from a genuine impulse towards violence on the part of the executioner and their purpose is not to provide unprincipled gratification for the audience. The Marquis de Sade was prosecuted for moderantism during the French Revolution and refused to exert his powers as magistrate and President of the Section des Piques to carry out the behests of the revolutionary tribunal, for sheer legal murder was not his idea of an authentic experience. As Simone de Beauvoir puts it, where no attempt to liberate emotion between man and man was involved, de Sade was not merely uninterested: he was disgusted.[8] Judicial cruelty was the exact opposite to his goal and his ideal.

The idea that the genuine has taken refuge in sin was not peculiar to de Sade in his time. Rameau's nephew, in Diderot's book of that name, warns us against virtue. First of all, virtuous people are unhappy, he tells us; you can tell by looking at them. Second, unhappy people make sure to make others unhappy; they are cruel; therefore, virtuous people are really a source of hidden cruelty in our society. What is still more harmful, virtuous people act from principles or notions of behaviour rather than from impulse; consequently, they act without sincerity.[9] The great value of evil is that it can never be insincere, and since the final value that must sustain all other values is sincerity, evil is the repository of the one inexpugnable value. As long as genuine evil has a place in the world, virtue, the basic virtue of honesty and sincerity, is safe. On the other hand, the wider the net of formal virtue spreads its toils, the greater the danger that all authentic experience will be suppressed, the fainter becomes the gleam of truth in our lives. Once again we recognize the Hell of the religious, as visualized by Blake.

What for Diderot was a moral aside was for de Sade an obsession. Again, we may suspect the quest for the recovery of a basic attribute of innocence, the ability to feel, behind de Sade's compulsion for violence. Where, someone may ask, is the evidence of a search for innocence in his beating a servant-girl on Easter Sunday, carving her up with a penknife, and pouring varieties of coloured wax into the wounds he had inflicted?[10] The reply might be that these are, at least, actual actions, resulting in real experiences; they are

motivated; their very extravagance bears witness to the gen-
uineness of the need that drove de Sade to carry them out;
whereas the tepid kindliness of some fairy-tale idyll, or the
sentimental benevolism which is its social form, are mere
hypocrisy. With truth lies virtue; and with virtue, innocence; and if the only remaining habitat of truth in our
lives is what we usually call perversion, we must roll up
our sleeves and dig for it there.

It is easy to confuse de Sade's morality with that of
Baudelaire or of Huysmans (*A Rebours*): but for de Sade sin
is not a rebellion against God that really signifies an in-
direct acknowledgment of God. It is not an inverted form
of grace but a direct expression of human desire, and for
that reason only is it precious. There is no question of
felix culpa here, no thought of setting up a feud with God
that has submission as its ultimate objective, as in Donne or
Herbert. In Baudelaire, too, as in de Sade, we are immersed
in sex and corruption, but we also have a penetration beyond to the central paradise; and the innocence available
in that world may ultimately be referred to the positive
category with which we began.

The Marquis de Sade is somewhat more akin to Blake and
to Nietzsche than to Baudelaire and the pseudo-Satanic
school. Blake's contribution to the theme has been too
thoroughly described to bear repeating, but Nietzsche still
yields many useful insights. For writers such as Blake and
Nietzsche it is not merely that innocence must first make a
detour through sin, as in Dante or in Milton; innocence has
to be regained by our recovering the capacity to experience.
Above all, the one way we must *not* try to recover innocence
is by turning our backs on experience, as Blake's Thel or
Valéry's Jeune Parque attempt to do.

The first step on the road to this form of innocence is
taken when we do away with the artificial, abstract cate-

gories of good and evil. Nietzsche harps on this theme as
regularly as does Blake. This arbitrary distinction between
good and bad that leads to the condemnation of a whole
province of human activity, without regard for the richness, the energy, and the truth it may contain, can rob us
of all our creative potential. We must first of all realize that
"What is done out of love always takes place beyond good
and evil." [11] The aesthetic, intellectual ascetic ideal and the
spiritual asceticism of the priest are related dangers, both
ways of damaging the life impulse. The priest is no apostle
of innocence; he is the sneaking serpent, the voice of cun-
ning, the insidious yet ferocious enemy of all life. He fosters
official morality and ethics; ethics, born of fear, and morality,
the poisoner of love. "What if morality," asks Nietzsche,
"should turn out to be the danger of dangers," a narcotic,
a temptation to sloth and decay.[12] The "good and the just,"
incapable of creation, endanger the whole human future:
the loathing engendered in us by the presence of their weakness in ourselves can drive us to self-extinction. All hope of
recovering our self-respect is a hope of recovering our desires,
our creative impulses, and our ability to feel: and these must
be accepted and approved wherever we find them. If they
are in war and violence, war and violence we must have.
Cruelty is one of the mainsprings of our being. The abstract
intellect itself, which violates our every desire through its
objectivity, does so only because of the pleasure we can
derive from this act of cruelty towards ourselves. As we
might expect, we find repeated in Nietzsche some of de
Sade's key principles; the murderer loves blood not booty,
and to deal with him either by cold, dispassionate justice or
with sentimental sympathy is an insult to his human dignity,
to that vital power that has found satisfaction and fulfilment
in his act. The watery innocence peddled by the official
moralists, the soulful idiots and the holy simpletons who

supposedly symbolize the consummation of the spiritual life, is for Nietzsche just one of the pathological stimulants of decadence, a sort of aphrodisiac of corruption.

We must, then, find our way back to what we really feel. *Zarathustra* echoes with the outcry against the false innocence that desires but acts not and with appeals for a return to the true. "Alas, what has happened to that deceiving innocence I once had, the innocence of good men and their noble lies!" [13] "Do I advise you to deaden your senses? I advise you to have inno-sense . . . how sweetly can the bitch sensuality beg for a piece of spirit if a piece of flesh is denied her." [14] Or again: "My brothers, why is the lion in the spirit necessary? Why does not the burden-bearing beast, which renounces and is reverent, suffice? . . . To create freedom and a reverent 'No' even in the face of duty: for this, my brothers, the lion is necessary . . . But tell me, my brothers, what can the child accomplish that even the lion cannot do? Why must the ravaging lion turn into a child?/ The child is innocence and forgetfulness, a new beginning, a game, a self-starting wheel, a prime motion, a reverent 'Yes.' " [15] Zarathustra himself is to become that child. " 'Oh Zarathustra, you shall go as the shadow of things to come: thus you shall command, and commanding, walk at the head.'/And I replied, 'I am ashamed.'/Then it said again without voice: 'You must become a child, without shame.' " [16] And in the end, doves and lion surround Zarathustra as he prepares to go forth to the world, like the morning sun, armed with what Nietzsche elsewhere calls that rarest thing on earth, the incomparable naïveté of a strong heart.

Some hint of the paradise awaiting us if we succeed in liberating our instinctual powers and in rediscovering the reality of our emotions is given by such spokesmen for the "new romanticism" as Norman O. Brown or Herbert Marcuse, for instance in the astonishingly optimistic *Eros and Civilization*. No longer used as a full-time instrument of labor, the body would again become an instrument of pleasure. Within transformed institutions, liberated from bondage to the "performance principle," the libido would come into its own. In such a situation, Marcuse envisages not a society of sex maniacs, but, on the contrary, the absorption and generalization of mere sexuality into all the normal activities of life, including work. "In this context," says Marcuse, "sexuality tends to its own sublimation." [17] Although Marcuse is not concerned with sources, we have here again, *mutatis mutandis,* the life of primitive man as described in Rousseau's *Discours sur les origines de l'inégalité;* the resemblance is especially distinct in the argument that violent manifestations of sexuality are only a product of repression, and that instinctual freedom provides a pacifying rather than an inflammatory medium for human behavior.[18] We seem to find ourselves back in the intellectual atmosphere of the eighteenth century.

The third and last conception of innocence I wish to consider presents a somewhat different pattern of ideas from those we have been reviewing. It would be well to remember that this idea of innocence has gone through the purgatory of Kafka and Heidegger, for whom no innocence in the ordinary human sense exists. It has had to battle against odds and to camouflage itself so effectively for survival that one can scarcely recognize it as innocence at all. To have run the gauntlet of existentialist theory and emerged alive, in whatever form, proves the pertinacity of the innocence principle. In Kafka's story, "The Penal Colony," the first law is that guilt is never to be doubted. All of us are criminals. At the sixth hour, after we have been sufficiently lacerated by the harrow, the meaning of our plight may dawn on us in a momentary recognition of our guilt that is our closest approach to innocence. (The idea that innocence becomes available only at the moment of death is nothing new, of course; it is the theme of Tolstoi's *Death of Ivan Ilyitch* and is perhaps an underlying idea of Milton's *Samson Agonistes* as well.) For Jean-Paul Sartre, the pursuit of a stable state of innocence is just one of the ways by which we try to escape from our *pour-soi* into an *en-soi,* to escape from our freedom into a fixed condition in which we will no longer have the responsibility of perpetual choice.[19] The opposite of guilt in Sartre's system is not innocence but involvement. But Martin Heidegger in our time has made the most damaging attack on the whole concept of innocence. Our first act of consciousness, for Heidegger, contains guilt in its essence. Insofar as we harbor the principle of inadequacy at all we are constantly guilty. Insufficient and terrified from the first moment of awareness, when we begin to cast about ourselves for a footing in the abyss, we immediately throw out artificial footholds and build up a network of apparent supports for our imperiled and indeed prematurely doomed consciousness. We create an artificial, pluralized, desperately loquacious self; we burrow into inauthenticity as our only refuge from the truth about our destiny. It takes death to wipe away the cobwebs of illusion and to return us to silence and ourselves: death, the only moment of truth, when man faces the night that is the symbol of his destiny: as Tiutchev had put it long before, "And in the strange, unfathomable night / He [man] recognizes his fateful inheritance." [20]

Where, then, is the chance for the survival of innocence if, on the contrary, our survival depends on an initial gesture of spurious hope and the creation of a bubble of inauthenticity about ourselves to supply a livable environment, before we stifle in the choking atmosphere of the absolute, as Joseph K. in Kafka's *Trial* stifles in the atmosphere of the court? And yet, ordered out the front door, innocence returns by another way: no longer in the positive form of Undine, no longer as the inmost heart of immorality and blasphemy as in de Sade or Baudelaire, but as a simple blank appraisal of the world as it is. It returns as Meursault, the hero of Camus' *L'Etranger*.

The ideal can no longer be defended even as myth or image: if we try to trot it out refurbished, as long as it can be recognized at all it will simply be laughed off the stage. Immoralism and violence too have grown boring, and we are past the inverted religiosity of Dostoyevsky. Even experience, in any vivid sense, seems simply untrue. If we cannot find what we want in the plain, flat surface of reality, if the drab, the colourless, will not yield us the elixir of innocence, then we may have to give up seeking this essence altogether.

The story of *L'Etranger,* which has already been sketched above, is familiar to almost all readers. We first meet the hero of the book, Meursault, when he is attending the funeral of his mother in a North African home for the aged. He shows no particular emotion about his mother's death and soon returns to the city where he promptly begins a liaison with a former typist from the office, Marie. When she asks him whether he loves her, he says no, but agrees to marry her at her suggestion. Through an unsought acquaintanceship with a neighbour of his who is a bit of a thug, Meursault becomes embroiled in a quarrel with some Arabs, which ends with his shooting one of them on the beach. His motive for the murder is not clear, even to himself; it is simply that as he approached the Arab the Arab drew a knife, which, without directly threatening Meursault, shot a keen ray of sunlight from its blade, searing his brain in a blinding flash that made him pull the trigger.

At the trial the main issue is not his murder of the Arab but his apparent lack of feeling for his mother. Meursault is condemned for his lack of humanity; not because he killed someone, but because he didn't cry at his mother's funeral. At the end, before his execution, he finally finds his footing,

and can face death with unflinching calm, even with enthusiasm, for he has understood the meaning of his life.
What he knew implicitly before has now become consciously
clear to him; that (as I have put it before) we must take
sides with the *outside,* that we must take up our position in
the surface of reality, in order to face and recognize our own
real situation, oriented from the beginning towards death
and conquering death by the rejection of the subjective role.
If we have never slipped into the evasiveness of idealism,
we can come to know ourselves in a sort of inverted pantheism, from the vantage-point of the mountains, and also come
to know the opaque, invulnerable mountain greatness in
ourselves.

Meursault, *l'étranger,* is too matter-of-fact to serve as the
innocent hero in either the positive or the negative sense.
His innocence is neither sweet nor bitter; neutral, dull, unaffected by any of the significant events that should punctuate
his existence, he seems to wander through a world with
which he has no close bonds of any sort. There is no involvement with anything in his experience. He is like a
piano with the dampers in perfect condition: there is absolutely no echo after any event, no resonance. Events sink
into him like pellets into a sandbag; they lead nowhere, they
have no further meaning. At his trial, the magistrate tells
him that the worst of sinners can obtain forgiveness if he will
repent and become like a little child, with a simple, truthful
heart. But Meursault is already that little child: and as far
as repentance is concerned, we soon learn that, like all truly
innocent heroes, he does not know the meaning of regret.
He has always been far too much absorbed in the present
moment to think back at all. In some ways he recalls the
peasant murderer in Andreyev's *Seven Who Were Hanged,*
but he is more articulate, and what he himself fails to express, Camus concludes for him in *The Myth of Sisyphus*
(chapter "La Liberté absurde.") The absurd man, like all

men, says Camus, is urged to recognize his guilt. But in a world without metaphysical dimensions, there can be no guilt. The absurd man feels himself innocent; in fact, all that he can feel is the weight of his irremediable innocence.

In simple terms, Meursault's innocence is plain truth. He is not prepared to tamper with his honesty for any result. He will not describe his dealings with his mother in words that will enable his judges to recognize him as a "human being" in their terms. We learn at the end of the book that he has indeed understood and loved his mother, implicitly before, explicitly now, but true love is a very difficult feeling to describe, words are inappropriate to convey it, and Meursault will not falsify the reality by reducing it to familiar phrases. The uncompromising precision of his description of experience, the refusal to add one jot of convention to the exact truth about his feelings, condemns him, but saves his world. Innocence has become the ability to see things as they are rather than in terms of an artificial scheme of values. To repeat: in a world where ideals have been proved to have no reality, reality is the only remaining ideal, and to rescue it from contamination by false ideals is the goal of the crusade undertaken by this strange new Knight of Innocence. Meursault's exalted standard of truth, his objectivity in a world where objectivity is the only remaining form of honour, commands respect; and it does more as well. His acceptance of things as they are enables him to reach a final confrontation with the meaning of his life and to achieve the purgation of hope. At this moment he realizes that he exists on the same level as the mountains, he achieves a sense of proud kinship with his mother, and he gains the freedom to declare before his execution, "I had been happy, and I was happy still." Reality has vindicated itself. Only he who has the innocence to know and recognize all things as they are, only he who rests in reality itself, without intellectualization or the imposition of values on his experiences, can trust the world to carry him through to a clear-eyed affirmation in the face of the absurd. Only he has the right to call himself happy.

In the rejection of systems and the high regard for the minute forms of truth that we find in Camus there is a curious resemblance to eighteenth-century scientific method, and by some circuitous route we seem once more to have rejoined the company of Diderot, the encyclopedists, and the idéologues. But a movement forward is harder to envisage. As it does for so many other ideas, *The Stranger* seems to mark the end of the road for the concept of innocence.

> The blood-dimmed tide is loosed, and everywhere
> The ceremony of innocence is drowned.
>
> Yeats, *The Second Coming*

Kierkegaard has said that once we have assumed sin, we can no longer go back to our normal lives without first having confronted the absolute in a sort of moral showdown: and having confronted the absolute, we would have neither the desire nor the means to resume our normal lives anyway.[21] A return to innocence seems forbidden by experience and philosophy alike. Perhaps we should stop trying and seek other values. But it is hard to give up the mirage of a return to our limpid primordial harmony. We can only hope that if there be no way back to it, there is something beyond it. Unfortunately, not everyone can be a Meursault.

❦ 5 ❧

The
Uncreating Word

"OLD FATHER CHAOS (as the poets call him) in these wild spaces reigns absolute, and upholds his realms of darkness. He presses hard upon our frontier, and one day, belike, shall by a furious inroad recover his lost right, conquer his rebel state, and reunite us to primitive discord and confusion."[1] The triumph of Chaos is detailed by Pope in *Dunciad* IV:

> As one by one, at dread Medea's strain,
> The sickening stars fade off th'ethereal plain;
> Lo! thy dread Empire, Chaos! is restored;
> Light dies before thy uncreating word:
> Thy hand, great Anarch! lets the curtain fall;
> And universal Darkness buries All.

In Pope's poem, the "uncreating word" is the word that undoes creation; it is the word that rolls the film of experience back off the reel of time. It is the answer to God's word, and it restores the silence before the beginning. It is also the word of aphasia, the word that allows us to sink back into the golden age before meaning had been invented, when Chaos (i.e. the world before concepts had reduced reality to a hand-list of trivia) was plenipotentiary, the King before the kings. It speaks of an innocence prior to the innocence of morality. Many authors make reference to Chaos with a mixture of fear and respect: he is not a mere Devil, a servile antithesis to a man-made God, confined in the categories of ethics. Hesiod, Empedocles, Milton, Blake, Yeats admire and stumble as they skirt a direct confrontation with this retiring but redoubtable antagonist; Shelley, in *Prometheus Unbound,* comes perhaps closest to finding a way of talking about him.

In this first sense, then, the "uncreating word" is very close indeed to the theme of this book, which deals with a return to silence and asks what may be found if we lift the corner of the leaf of words. ". . . truth does not need formulae to exist; it is linked with the real, which is by nature mute." [2] While we persist in our attempts to know only through definition and language, we keep ourselves at a hopeless distance from reality, which is always at an infinite remove from our speech. To quote another plea for ignorance (Nicholas of Cusa, *De Docta Ignorantia*), "Solomon, the Wise, affirmed that in all things there are difficulties which beggar explanation in words . . . even the most profound Aristotle in his First Philosophy affirms it to be true of the things most evident to us in nature—then in presence of such difficulty we may be compared to owls trying to look at the sun . . ." [3]

On the other hand, if we take the phrase "the uncreating word" out of Pope's context and interpret it naïvely as "the word that does not create," we are still in the midst of our topic, for it has been one of my postulates that we do not make things up with words but make words up from things. Lest this sound like a denial of the imagination, I must make it clear that I take "things" to be not only objects, but experiences; I am not denying the substantiality of the imagination, but I am saying that the quality of an imaginative experience precedes its mutation into words; [4] and again Pope's phrase is an appropriate motto.

So far is my position from a denial of the imagination that I shall eventually argue that imaginative writing has suffered equally with descriptive writing in the complex change of verbal functions that has been taking place over the past century. For the present I merely wish to emphasize the limitations of language; language in one of its forms is dying, and, as I have contended in my introduction, in its death-throes it has become megalomaniac and paranoid. Through its political agency, linguistics, it is laying claim to wider and wider territories in the intellectual universe, and beyond: for instance, the linguists go so far as to argue that the resemblance of the genetic code to a communications system is more than fortuitous. [5] The feeling grows apace that whatever cannot be dealt with in linguistic terms is not worth dealing with at all. Yet this conviction results from the reduction of language to a set of instructions for programming and from the assumption that whatever is not available to such description is of no importance and can be ignored. The useless side of language has been forgotten, but the current conception of language is appropriate only for the new language, which is a non-language, merely a set of grunts, gestures, clicks or clacks that will produce an immediate specifiable result. By the time a theory has been elaborated that will do justice to the more complex language of the past, the raw material for such a theory will have disappeared, and there will be nothing on which to frame a theory, any more than we can frame a theory on the sensibility of the Great Auk.

It is natural to expect that linguistic theories can cover all contingencies, when the "language" of which we are thinking is a set of instructions for action under finite conditions. Like the language which scientists have proposed to teach to chimpanzees, it anticipates a prior restriction in the range of our experiences.[6] This limitation in the way we conceive of it confers a curious independence on language. It is neither historical (a system oriented towards action and production does not record experiences for the sake of recording them, or dally with the past) nor speculative, descriptive, or imaginative; it begins and ends in itself. It is a kind of minimum instrument that does its job, but is unrelated to either its user or its object. Squat and self-sufficient, it inspires curiosity, rather than love or interest. By the time we reach the half-century in literature, a hypocritical posture has been adopted: writers like Camus have surrendered to this language while pretending that they express themselves only accidentally, left-handedly, as though they were not really using language at all. But it is more interesting to consider the early development of this idiom among authors of the decadent tradition, such as Huysmans, who could still confuse arbitrariness with ornament; in Stefan George; or in Rimbaud.[7] Rimbaud is obviously caught between two incompatible solutions to the problem of representation and tries to apply both at once. On the one hand he attempts, by an extreme emphasis on the detached and "illuminated" object, to make one forget the word that designates it and to produce an experience of apparently unmediated perception. In other words, he tries to make his words vanish. (Of course, with the words, the author presumably vanishes too.) On the other hand, by weighing all his linguistic anchors, he simultaneously creates an impression of arbitrariness, so that his words seem to relate neither to each other in a coherent texture nor to a recognizable series of experiences. There is a sense of detachment about his language that makes one feel it is an insult to ask him what he means, at the same time as the words attempt to disappear in the effulgence of an alinguistic world. From one side we appear to be dealing with pure objects; from the other, with unrelated words.

The most intriguing of these authors who first encountered on their path the new language, in which words have officially declared their freedom from user and purpose alike, and who set out to make deliberate artistic use of it, was Raymond Roussel. Roussel's situations are totally arbitrary, but instead of filling them in with a neutral, colorless substance appropriate to their emptiness of meaning, he chooses to work them out in the most exotic medium he can provide. The *Impressions d'Afrique* proceeds as though it were feeding passion fruit to robots: the pointless situation is forced to the drinking-trough, so to speak, and under our eyes it swells and becomes real with a new and unique reality as it is compelled to sup huge draughts of highly colored, richly textured immediacy, as improbable as itself but irresistibly concrete. Like Roussel's horse, Romulus, that has been obliged to learn to talk, it finally wanders off, outraged but ambulatory, "still murmuring vague reflections." [8] It is as though Camus' intellectual instrumentation were being applied to the universe of the Douanier Rousseau. The Rube Goldberg mechanisms of the industrial imagination are nourished with a material that is the contrary of their natural banausic diet. Roussel's tireless technological fantasy elaborates machine after machine, each more weird and complex than the last. But this frenzied activity is all pun, it is all in the service of word-play; and its entire realm is that thin line of stasis produced by the collision of an immovable object with an irresistible force: the dead word and the real world. There is a sense of stalemate in Roussel's best scenes, a sense of unrepeatable perfection. In each case, the meaningless has been forced to confess a meaning.

Before the death of language announced itself in a form sufficiently distinct to prompt authors to deal with it, each in his own way,[9] we can see certain dimensions of language lose their depth, or atrophy, as the purpose of language becomes more narrowly defined. Rimbaud says the devil likes books that neither teach nor describe; [10] and I have remarked previously that in fully functional language there is no room for simple description. In Gerard Manley Hopkins' notebooks we have the last great descriptive document in English. It marks the end of a tradition that had been carried from John Ray and Gilbert White down through Darwin's *Voyage of the Beagle* and Melville's *The Encantadas*. And even Hopkins' notebooks seem as much an agonized struggle to capture and hold the freshness of perception, with the aid of concepts and a magnifying focus, as the record of a vision that is naturally filled. The fatal sophistication in Hopkins, the touch of just-too-muchness in his words, rob one of the sense of fulfillment and make one wonder what he is really trying to say. His words go out in pursuit of reality like falcons stooping to the kill: and there is a destructive effect in the contact, a bruising on impact that leaves the object stunned with the force of the word. The poetic perception that Arnold describes in his essay on Maurice de Guérin does not, after all, occur in Hopkins: we do not feel ourselves to be "no longer bewildered and oppressed" by objects, "but to have their secret, and to be in harmony with them . . ." Ultimately, Hopkins does not seem to have much confidence in either his words or his objects, and sets his words repeatedly at the throat of reality in a kind of desperate effort to learn something from the assault, almost like Counsellor Krespel seeking the source of music by dismembering violins. I should like to suggest that this hope of impounding reality in words, of getting at the whole thing through description, is a mistake: as Francis Ponge says, the point is rather "to keep returning to the object itself, to

what is raw in it, *different:* and in particular to what is
different from what I have just said about it." [11] Perhaps, as
I shall propose later, the hope for language lies in its reaching into reality and making a province for itself there, rather
than in seizing reality and trying to hold it down. It is hard
to avoid accusing Hopkins of a certain poetic pride that is
also his poetic weakness; as though in his effort to copy creation he came to think that language might actually achieve
something comparable to the Word. Great as is Hopkins'
achievement, he is clearly wrong in thinking that a thing or
event can be so fully captured in words that they alone will
suffice to recreate the experience; it is this assumption that
words can do more than they can that gives us the measure
of Hopkins' ambition and also the nature of his failure.
Words cluster around an experience, they do not inhabit it:
and a cluster of words must still have the stem of experience
in it for the experience to be real. In any case, in Hopkins'
notebooks the effort of description is carried to an extreme,
as far as Hopkins was able to conceive of it: to the burning
margin of one kind of language.

One cannot, of course, rest a great deal upon any one case:
what Hopkins did not do cannot delimit what others may;
a boundary, no matter how compendious, is not a horizon.
The *Notebooks* serve my argument as paradigm rather than
as sufficient historical or predictive evidence. Hopkins tried
to rescue reality for language through a certain kind of
description. Although in my view, this effort could not be
successful, and through its very strenuousness implies an
admission of loss, the attempt necessarily commands our
admiration. But as language becomes instructional rather
than representational, its descriptive activity must grow
weaker. (Here, I should say, I am in complete agreement
with Foucault concerning the end of representation as a
linguistic function, and the substitution of a sign-system
which is strictly subservient to action: "We talk because we

act, not because in recognizing we know.") [12] With the withering of description—and this is the point I have been trying to make—an element of imagination drops off as well. It is true that a pretense of maintaining both is preserved in the pseudo-description of the objectivists (Ponge, Robbe-Grillet, etc.) and the pseudo-imagination of the surrealists (e.g. Kenneth Koch) in a kind of Wordsworth-Coleridge division of the poetic empire; but such polarization preserves nothing of experience. I believe that together with the decline of description, there has been not only a general loss to the verbal imagination, but that at least one of its components has vanished entirely.

In a way, what I am about to discuss is too obvious. We do not have to be reminded that we live in an industrial age, which began to achieve overpowering momentum in the second half of the nineteenth century; its effect was early enough defined and sensitively described by those, such as Alfred de Vigny or Henry Adams, who accompanied it into its majority. The consequent "dissociation of sensibility" and loss of hold upon reality have been repeatedly expounded to us in the commentaries of T. S. Eliot and Allen Tate, though no great improvement on Kierkegaard's wording has been achieved: after Kant, he said, "The ego was like the crow, which, deceived by the fox's praise of its person, lost the cheese." [13] I offer no discovery in this field, unless it be the discovery of my own anachronistically pristine reactions to a hackneyed predicament. If there is any departure from commonplace opinion in my argument, it is only in the claim that specimens of a kind of pre-lapsarian use of language can still be found at the end of the nineteenth century; that they are more readily identified in a branch of popular journalism than in recognized literature; and that these examples express not merely a naïvely and unconsciously "undissociated" mental process, but a genuine creative moment in which language and reality thrust towards a single object. As Schiller once said, "It is this kind of expression, in which the sign disappears completely into the referent, . . . that is identified above all others with literary genius." [14] The phenomenon, or rather the expression which it achieved in the journalistic medium, is of slight importance for literature; yet its unavailability to us (if it is indeed unavailable—and one cannot, of course, prove a negative) is symptomatic of a deficiency in the contemporary imagination that is pervasive and significant. One would hardly argue that the imagination has expired in the twentieth century; but one of its fins has atrophied, so that it is condemned henceforth to paddle a little laboriously and askew. There is one very minor sense in which the word *can* create, and it is this capacity of language that has been lost. If language cannot make something in the full sense of the word, it can at least grope within reality for a realm of its own, in which it in a way creates what is. But Shelley's declaration that poetry should compel us to imagine what we know has become the most difficult demand in aesthetics for us to understand. What we know, now, we know, and that is all there is to it. But not very long ago, it was not so clear that to know was simply to stop something dead in its tracks; knowledge did not yet possess that deadly Midas-touch, and it was still possible to play within the realm of truth. It was once possible to treat real events as though they were a story; now we know they can only be facts.

The field of writing on which I wish to draw for illustrations of this aspect of expression is not within literature proper. It is not a literary phenomenon as such but a way of thinking or attitude of mind, and its characteristic tone emerges for me most distinctly from late nineteenth-century magazine articles and popular scientific literature. Beneath comparison with the descriptive style of a Hopkins, it yet possesses some features which his more sophisticated sensibility lacks. One finds it in children's geographical manuals, elementary biology textbooks of the 1890's (written in dialogue form but framed on a complete Latin taxonomy), fishing stories, encyclopedia articles, summaries of popular knowledge about heaven, earth, or sea, travelogues, "animal kingdoms," the whole medley of information and action compiled in series with titles such as *Travel and Adventure, The Water World, The Outdoor Library,* and so forth. As it happens, one section of an *Encyclopédie d'histoire naturelle* by a certain Dr. Chenu, describing the flight of starlings, was canonized by Lautréamont: quoted verbatim and without acknowledgment, it became a key passage in the *Chants de Maldoror,* and as such was extravagantly praised by no less a connoisseur than Maurice Blanchot, apparently unaware of its source. But most of this material was destined for the tables outside country bookshops; and soon afterward its themes, subtly but fatally transmuted, were turned into the sluices of *National Geographic, Field and Stream,* and the other new semi-scientific or sporting magazines. But what sort of elixir can one hope to distill from such an unpromising mash?

The advantage of all this semi-informational, semi-realistic exploration of the surfaces and recesses of our world was its margin of ignorance and its margin of impotence. The language in which it was couched did not have to fear that it might be called on at any moment to put a half-Nelson on the universe, or that the discoveries it reported would be fed into a functional scheme that presumed to set the boundaries of nature. It was genuinely exploratory, in the sense that it was sure it would never reach a destination that would make further questioning seem less speculative. Man's goals had not yet been brought within his reach. It was a language that had confidence in the inability of man and his instruments ever to achieve anything of consequence; it could play with nature, because the thought of controlling nature never arose seriously. This confidence of language in its own futility preserved a whole dimension for it that the language of modern communications, condemned to perpetual responsibility, or even the aesthetic-theological tool of Hopkins' inner science, could never have. Such a language had a special freedom, for it could act with the assurance that it would never have to be turned to a real use. A language that can never be useful for purposes beyond itself can be of use to itself, it can move within reality without usurping or evading it. The art of nineteenth-century faunal illustration, both more circumstantial and more extravagant than the later work that expects to be compared with routine photography, has much of this character, in its weird realism of noddy terns, curled-crested phalarises, and common seals.[15]

It is very difficult to illustrate this sort of quality in writing by quotation, since what we are dealing with is not "literature," and it cannot be quoted like lines of poetry. The effect it produces is a matter of its assumptions rather than of its style, and is felt in the mass rather than in the individual passage: indeed, to cite single passages is likely to create a somewhat ludicrous effect, and I am in the awkward position of having to make claims for a literary essence for which I cannot provide an adequate body of quotation. But some of the real-adventure stories of the 1890's go from a frame of history to anecdote to description to something that does transcend all of these. The élan of language that is free from the bondage of achievement carries it off the top of reality where for a moment we hang suspended in language alone, as in a cage that has revealed its inner space. Here words show that they can set up their own world in the midst of the world of things. Language picks up the suggestions of reality and carries them through its own momentum beyond themselves, suspending them in itself, so that things show the translucency of thoughts, while the words with their clear walls sustain the mirage. Indeed many of the numerous descriptions of mirages from these books communicate a similar effect: "The entire horizon was lifting and doubling itself continually, and objects at a great distance beyond it rose, as if by strange enchantment, and stood suspended in the air . . ." [16] The language in which these events take place tends to be slightly genteel, slightly generalized; it has a penchant for the present historic tense; but it can have instress without stress, and inscape that does not have to fear lest it be turned to escape. Kitty, the heroine of Howells' *A Chance Acquaintance* (Boston, 1873), encounters the new experience of Quebec City in this way. Everything is as real as if it were a story. The *real* figures in the convent garden "were but figures in a beautiful picture of something old and poetical; but she loved them . . . and was most happy in them, the same as if they had been real." (p. 92) ". . . she unerringly relegated" each of the people in the streets "to an appropriate corner of her world of unreality" (p. 97). "So she went on turning substance into shadow, unless, indeed, flesh and blood is the illusion . . ." (p. 98).[17]

A typical introductory sentence from one of these adventure stories will read: "About one hundred miles north from Quebec lies Lake St. John, some twenty-six miles long by twenty wide." [18] It is as though a problem in ontology were being translated into a problem in arithmetic; but what in Melville would be the expression of a metaphysical attitude is here merely an experience of reality. The distances and dimensions would not be given so specifically if the question being asked were not "Can you tell me the essence of this phenomenon?" There is no answer to that question—it is in fact rhetorical—but at least by being specific about the dimensions of a physical thing relating to the essence, by the painstaking measurement of the phenomenon, we are doing justice to the essence, affirming its reality indirectly. The first step in the answer, the "No," is elided, because it would not be entirely true. Something about the essence can be told, and, although we cannot be specific about it, we can be specific about the next thing to it.

The syntax of the sentence, beginning with an inversion, places the distance from the point of reference before the point of reference itself, disorienting the reader and setting him (despite the precision of the topographical measurement) in an undefined space, about which the only certain feeling is that it is far from anything else. From this initial sense of dislocation and remoteness we move into expanding vistas of still more unmanageable distances, as the author follows out the rivers in the watershed of which the lake is the gathering-point. The movement outward continues, through a series of sentences of great length and powerful momentum, in a tone of generalization that sounds in part like a geography textbook, in part like a tourist guide, and in part like the expression of genuine awe.

> Fed by innumerable lakes and streams, most of these rivers are large. Three of them—the Ashuapmouchouan, "the river where they watch the moose," the Mistassini, or "river of the great rock," and the Peribonca, "the curious river"—come from great lakes on the summit of the watershed between the St. Lawrence and Hudson's Bay, receive large tributaries, are from 200 to 250 miles long, and are over a mile wide at their mouths, which are close together at the north-western end of the lake . . . This immense volume of water . . . has but one outlet, divided for the first eight miles into two branches by Alma Island, at the foot of which the Grande Décharge, after a circuit of twelve miles in mighty rapids, unites with the Petite Décharge— straighter, and held in check by dams for the safe passage of timber—to form La Décharge du Lac St. Jean, a mighty stream, which, after a turbulent course of some thirty miles more, wrenches asunder the syenite at Les Terres Rompues, seven miles above Chicoutimi, and expanding into fjord-like reaches, becomes the Saguenay.

"Near the lake the scenery is tame; but beyond the boundaries of the prehistoric sea . . ." and so on (pp. 27–28). The style is pedestrian, declarative, but there is the faintest echo of the questions in the *Book of Job* about it. Although as remote as possible from epic itself, it obviously thinks of itself as dealing with the backdrop of some universal epic. Statements about this kind of world must be made in generalized terms ("immense volume," "mighty stream," "prehistoric sea," etc.) because it is clearly beyond the measure of specification except at the unpretentious level of arithmetical numbers.

The same declarative, generalized style becomes more insistent, almost hammering, in the description of the Nipigon River.

> Some of the chutes of the Nepigon, as those that perpetually weave and tear to pieces Cameron's and Hamilton's Pools, and the thundering outrush of Lake Emma, are unapproachable by keels risking either upward or downward progress. Others, like the great rapid at Camp Minor, pulsing convulsed with the last water-spasm of Virgin Falls, a mile above it, may safely sweep the birch as it leaps skirting down one edge, taking dashes of foam inboard; but they roll with a weight and power that bar return . . . At other reaches, the river, just doubting whether it shall burst into a rapid, courses bold and strong in curling ripples, all on the point of dashing into foam, four or five feet deep across its whole breadth, over an even bottom of stones, more than pebbles and less than boulders, whirling the canoe smoothly a mile or more on level keel. (pp. 91–92)

It is hard to tell, in such passages, whether the events are inhabiting the language or the language actually subsumes the events.

> The cataract of Virgin Falls is striking for the grace and flow of its curves, both vertical and cross-sweeping; for the snowy dazzle flashing out of solid blue, just as it leaves the lip, into a storm of tossing pearls; for the mass of

water rushing in across from the western verge, beating half
the main flood aside; and for the lessening surges cresting
the blended torrents as they seethe away for half a mile
through a broad basin rimmed with green, and propor-
tioned in nature's nicest measure to the height of the fall.
In this font of fretted ivory and jewelled spray, the river
Nepigon receives its baptism.

From its leap out of the lake the river runs nearly due
south thirty-two miles, with a fall of three hundred and
thirteen feet, to Lake Superior. It pours a full, strong current—in many places sixty feet deep and two hundred wide
—clean up to its shores, without swamp or snag or drift.
(p. 90)

Especially in the first paragraph, there is an equalization
of language and events that leaves unconsidered the primacy
of either. Pure phenomenon—"snowy dazzle flashing out of
solid blue"—(notice the avoidance of mention of water,
foam, or any substantive referent) is the same as pure idea
—since the dazzle and the blue are what we see, and do not
pass through translation into any neutral term such as
"water," which is *not* what we see at the lip of the fall. At
this point, language has the same freedom and vigor of
existence as reality, and we can see the passage as either pure
generalized language or as a description of a thing; to repeat,
by telling what actually is so as if it were a story, the passage
enables things to enter and inhabit the realm of language.
The baptismal font of the Nipigon is also the basin of the
mind.

In the Saguenay there is no reason why the fish should
not go to the sea; in fact, they do descend to the tideway
in large numbers every spring with the heavy floods, but
whether they remount is as yet undetermined . . . but we
are inclined to think they return to spawn in the Décharge.
Stray individuals have been caught in the Saguenay Rivers,
at Tadoussac, and even in the St. Lawrence above the

Saguenay; but they are the exception . . . This statement
must be now modified. In 1889 Mr. Creighton observed
them in the Musquarro . . . (p. 35)

Of course what is all-important is the not-quite-knowing the
fishes' habits; and not expecting ever fully to know. The
style is only half natural history; in a subtler and soberer
sense than in Melville, the generative ethos that creates this
style is that what is contains a dimension of what-might-be
which really *contains* what is. What is is possible at the same
time that it is real: the possible and the potential are as
much the reality in the real as the real in it is. To quote
Husserl: "The old ontological doctrine that the knowledge
of possibilities must precede that of realities is . . . a great
truth." Heidegger puts it more simply: "Possibility stands
higher than reality." [19]

It would not be difficult to quote other passages that have
more claim to simple stylistic force and value; but I am not
trying to accumulate an anthology of the "beauties" of late
nineteenth century sporting literature, or even to identify
its general aesthetic features; I am only interested in isolating a single quality in this writing that is no longer available
to us. It is not, finally, a picturesque style; it is translucent
and offers a bareness of tone to match the translucence of its
subject-matter. It is significant that one of our authors declares the northern landscape to be worthless for the artist.
There is nothing in it that arrests the eye; it is essentially
toneless and lacks singularity of detail. The ubiquitous rock
is "little relieved by the trees . . . principally dense curtains
of spindling birch," and the occasional colorless willow.

Now and then a swift breeze, lifting the under-surface of
these leafy hillside masses, strikes a sudden note of ashen
gray, like a discord, into the landscape. If he turns to the
water, it offers still less to invite the brush. It flashes a tint
of steely blue, shot with foamy streaks and sparkles; and

even where in quiet deeps it wins a hue of turquoise green, there always lacks the rich brown and raisin-red color-gamut of eastern rivers flowing out of spruce forests. Momentary effects may be caught among these blues and grays—but they are bodiless and elusive—a fluid flame like . . . molten beryl . . . or the phosphorescent flicker before a storm. (pp. 116–17)

This is not the striking effect of "visionary dreariness;" frail as the example may be, this is the movement towards pure translucency, when the world's paleness, the unaccidented Absolute, is invoked by language that can then claim to have created its nameless, unaccidented object. To call on the absolute is to create it, since the content of what has been called forth cannot be specified; as it is named, language alone sustains it. In this sense, the naming of the element of the absolute *amidst* reality is the creation of an enclave in which language can be said to create, a privileged region in which things do not come before words.

The potential in the actual; the quality of the general in the specific; the equalization of event and word; for one last moment language could create what it saw, could imagine what it knew. At the fatal line before the arrival of the earth-movers, there was a concentration and accumulation of a vision of reality that has not been available since, as though just before the subjection of the world to the machine we had been granted one last moment of lucidity. But beyond this point reality is best left to itself. It is not true, as Hillis Miller would have it, that the authors of the twentieth century are "poets of reality." If we have lost our reality, words will not bring it back to us. In fact, such words as we have at our disposal can only serve to widen the gap.

No doubt it is not necessary for us to recapture only the particular creative essence I have been trying to describe in order to use language profitably, keenly though we may feel

the loss of that essence. In fact, to strive for some particular
mental posture is a strained tactic, not sufficiently generous
to the variety of our lives, which can presumably meet experience over a broad front and do not demand a single prerequisite for a comprehensive response. Nor would it be con-
sistent with my objections to simple periodization if I were
to deny the future any expectation of continuity with the
past. In the longer perspective, as one tries to transcend the
pessimism of the historical moment, the relation of language
with reality does not seem entirely hopeless. Some changes
will be necessary, but they are not changes that must bring
us back to the kind of language I have just been describing;
and they will be the natural consequence of the termination
of a cycle rather than the result of our deliberate act. For one
thing, the heritage of Wordsworth, in which the observer is
disparaged in favor of the percept, may have to be abandoned. The progression from Wordsworth via the half-way
house of Impressionism, the detached particulars of Rimbaud
and the Surrealists, through Ponge and Robbe-Grillet
through unnamability, though heralded as the ultimate con-
quest of the pathetic fallacy, may also be understood as a
general abdication of our ego-responsibility towards the
world. Robbe-Grillet's novels are a spelling out of the implicit deadness in Wordsworth: passivity is not total recep-
tivity, and the object that is not fully absorbed by consciousness or reverie, like St. Julian's beasts, becomes detached,
rebellious, and eventually menacing. As Hopkins says, it is
just that thing which produces a dead impression, "which
the mind . . . has made nothing of and has brought into
no scaping," that forces itself up in this way afterwards.[20] It
has been abused; it demands to participate in our lives; it
must have a name.

We can even understand that some critics would reject the
whole of the late preoccupation with "objects" as ridiculous.
There is always something lacking in all the talk about

"things." Even if one lets oneself become completely transparent to the world of things, what comes through is partly dead. The talk of objects must remain unsatisfying because even if they reach one fully they are still only objects. There is another kind of response to the world, and particularly to landscape, that one might associate with the name of Emily Brontë, though not with many more recent authors. Although it brings with it the fallacies of another extreme, it has the salutary effect of putting the emphasis back where it belongs, on the relationship between the observer and the object, instead of directing attention to the object alone. This approach presumes that the primary world is one to which the natural world is subordinated, that does not allow the natural world to assert itself or even to exist, that is in absolute conflict with it and annihilates it. It is the world of love into which the natural world is transfigured, and the experience of it is the opposite of passive, the opposite of an act of self-neutralization in favor of the neutrality of the natural world. It is neutral on neither half: the world becomes the dialogue of lovers.

Even St.-Jean Perse's formula of the "même espace poétique" (see above, p. 58), the domain in which the creative and the receptive are reconciled, is inadequate in these terms because it represents an attempt to come to terms with objects, as though objects were of such great significance, and could ever yield one important returns, even under the best of conditions. From the extreme view, all is eros,[21] and the sooner one sees the world as the tympanum of love, the better; we must get over the idea that the world is anything of much value "as is." From this point of view Wordsworth is wrong, and those who follow in his tradition are tame and fearful—and finally one ends up with the perversion of a Robbe-Grillet, natural offspring of Rousseau and Wordsworth and the school of passivity-to-nature. Yet for those who could not, or cannot, make the world vibrate, to "let the world reach them" was necessarily the greatest possible achievement; although it reached them, finally, not in its most vital but in a half-neutral form, so that the world they spoke of came to seem more and more inert.

But one may not have to believe with Blake, Brown, and Marcuse that a more vigorous attitude towards life (or, with Foucault and the school of Artaud, a more brutal attitude) will eventually redeem language. One may not even have to share Georges Bataille's hope that it may be within the means of the very culprit, of language as such, to regain for us access to the "souverain silence."[22] Even if we do not think that reality yields itself completely only when *we* bring it to life, we can still recognize a demand in reality for some sort of reciprocal response.[23] One might say that reality itself contains reserves with which language may one day have to have its rendezvous.

Unnamability is not the last word on the attempt of language to deal with things. On the one hand, reality is constantly exposing the inadequacy of our categories and reminding us that we cannot confine it or create it with words. On the other hand, it also seems to offer a perpetual temptation or invitation to our response. There is something like a generative activity within reality that calls for our recognition, that draws us out to reach towards it. I have been saying that words cannot create, and that in some sense they cannot even describe, since a structure of abstractions cannot exhaust any reality. It is generally acknowledged that under the best of circumstances, though words may arise from an experience of reality, this is not a reciprocal relation and we cannot move back with an equal sureness from words to the things they once presumably spoke about.[24] The intuitive process of language-generation obviously has a much more organic involvement with reality than the language structure once generated has to its semantic objects. Nevertheless, the object of language—let us call it reality—contains an element that does show a kinship with language. In this border-area of reality something goes on that has an affinity with the language process and that even calls on language for a reply. It is what we might call an area of implicit categories, a kind of middle ground between the category and the formless *Ding-an-sich*. It is true that no words will seize reality and pin it down for us or tell us what we see; on the other hand, what we see has a kind of internal structure that does not wait for words in order to assert its form. To quote Derrida: "S'il faut dire, avec Schelling, que 'tout n'est que Dionysos,' il faut savoir . . . que comme la force pure, Dionysos est travaillé par la différence. Il voit et se laisse voir." [25] The world does not consist of an amorphous *Ding-an-sich* on the one hand and the formal patterns of concept on the other, trying with futile repeated casts of the net to catch some fragment of faceless chaos. As I have suggested with reference to Chateaubriand's descriptions, the world consists of words that issue repeatedly in the attempt to relate to something that is itself in a state of organization, although its patterns just do not happen to correspond to the patterns of words. It is as though the chaos of the mind and the chaos of reality had parallel borders of organization, though not necessarily of the same character, that face each other. In his chapter on the concept of chaos Heidegger uses the metaphor of the stream to suggest the possibility of mediation between the two. ". . . that which can be known and that which knows determine themselves together . . . We must not divide the two and then seek to encounter them divided. Knowing is not like a bridge, which subsequently and occasionally joins the two already existing banks of a stream, but it is itself a stream, that creates the banks by its streaming, and that turns these banks *towards* each other in a more originative way than any bridge can do." [26] To recur to my own metaphor: in reverie these borders of organization that confront each other fade, or are passed over, and one latency seems to come into direct contact with the other; but perhaps only in the state of mind that accompanies artistic creation do the two borders coincide fully, so that the patterns of thought meet and become precisely identical with the patterns of reality. In the words of Schopenhauer, "only when subject and object reciprocally fill and penetrate each other completely does the adequate objectivity of Will, the true world as Vorstellung (Imagination) arise." [27] In any case, pre-linguistic reality is itself variegated and filled with organizational and self-dissolving activity which, if not a part of ourselves, at least tempts our response and contributes to the ground of ourselves; it contains forms that rise and subside; it is not a totally alien and undifferentiated spiritual substance or uniform God. In the latent there is order; it is not the order that an independent, arrogant yet functionally servile language displays; but as long as it is there, it is an invitation for a humbler language to renew its compact with reality and learn once more to obey the natural forms of the world. If such a reconciliation could take place, we might no longer have to feel that our only refuge from pride or falsehood lies in silence.

Notes

1. INTRODUCTION

1. Tiutchev: "A thought when spoken is a lie." Cf. Camus, "Sur une philosophie de l'expression": "Il s'agit de savoir si notre langue est mensonge ou vérité." ("It's a matter of deciding whether our language is lie or truth.")

The alienation of words from reality is the subject of Michel Foucault's *Les Mots et les choses* (Paris, 1966). Foucault thinks of the unity of the two as prevailing until the Renaissance, simply by virtue of a kind of primitive identification of signs and things. (Cf. John W. M. Verhaar, *Some Relations between Language, Speech, and Thought* [Assen, 1963], pp. 78–79). I believe that the unity is not necessarily of this simple nature, should be recoverable from almost any linguistic act, and is not an archaeological curiosity bound to a particular historical epoch: I would agree that ". . . il doit exister, en effet, une vérité qui est de l'ordre de l'objet" and at the same time "de l'ordre du discours. . . ." (Foucault, p. 331. "Somewhere there does have to be a truth which is of the order of the object" and at the same time "of the order of expression.")

2. See, for instance, L. S. Dembo, *Conceptions of Reality in Modern American Poetry* (Berkeley and Los Angeles, 1966). Several of the ideas in my introduction are similar to the observations of John V. Hagopian in "Symbol and Metaphor in the Transformation of Reality into Art," *Comparative Literature,* XX (Winter, 1968), 45–54, which appeared shortly after this was written.

3. For instance, Benjamin Lee Whorf; see also J. Lohmann, "Das Verhältnis des abendländischen Menschen zur Sprache (Bewusstsein und unbewusste Form der Rede)," *Lexis,* III (1952), 5–49, especially p. 35.

4. Martin Heidegger, *Sein und Zeit* (Tübingen, 1963), p. 60.

5. Ibid., p. 109.

6. *Pour un nouveau roman* (Paris, 1963), p. 176. Of course
Robbe-Grillet would be the first to acknowledge that one does
not experience the "things" he writes about as real, though the
reader's reservations may not fall in the area where the author
expects them to. Obviously Robbe-Grillet's objects seem to
control one too fully, and precisely because there is no give and
take in our interaction with them, they are not felt to be part
of experience. They are too detached and assertive to be rooted
in nature. But what this quality leads to is finally that the pure
object comes to be felt as the bare word, in a much starker
sense than a fantastic, romantic, or merely unconvincing description could be. Cf. Jacques Derrida, *L'Ecriture et la différence* (Paris, 1967), p. 18, on Artaud: "Car la pensée de la chose
comme *ce qu'elle est* se confond déjà avec l'expérience de la
pure parole." ("For the thought of the thing as that *which it is*
already becomes indistinguishable from the experience of the
purely verbal.")

Hegel seems to have foreseen the invasion of the aesthetic
experience by objects in the late phase of Romantic art, which
re-admits common externality in a kind of final demonstration
that all externalizations are equally useless (*Vorlesungen über
die Aesthetik* [Stuttgart-Bad Cannstatt, 1964], II, 133–134). "It
interweaves its inner being with the accidentality of external
forms. . . . Romantic art allows externality free rein again, and
(with this view) permits any and every sort of material, down
to flowers or trees or the most ordinary household articles, to
enter indiscriminately into its representation, even in the natural
contingency of their existence as objects." Since this translation
may be disputed at some points, I give the original: "sie verwebt
ihr Inneres auch mit der Zufälligkeit der äusseren Bildung . . .
[Eben deshalb aber] lässt die romantische Kunst die Aeusser-
lichkeit [sic] sich nun auch ihrer Seits wieder frei für sich ergehn,
und erlaubt in dieser Rücksicht allem und jedem Stoff, bis auf
Blumen, Bäume und gewöhnlichste Hausgeräthe herunter, auch
in der natürlichen Zufälligkeit des Daseyns ungehindert in die
Darstellung einzutreten."

7. Wilhelm von Humboldt has an interesting if cryptic remark that is pertinent in *Über die Verschiedenheit des menschlichen Sprachbaues* (Bonn, 1960 facsim. of 1836 ed.), p. lxxix: "Was aus dem stammt, welches eigentlich mit mir Eins ist, darin gehen die Begriffe des Subjects und Objects, der Abhängigkeit und Unabhängigkeit in einander über." ("Whatever it is that takes its source in something that is really one with myself, in that, the notions of subject and object, dependence and independence, dissolve into each other.")

8. A characteristic statement of recent hermeneutics is quoted in Hans Jonas, *The Phenomenon of Life* (New York, 1966), p. 246. "This is true of theology as well . . . our answer to the call of revelation is linguistic. . . . Existence itself [is] essentially linguistic." A similar attitude governs, say, E. H. Gombrich's understanding of pictorial art in *Art and Illusion*. A portrait does not body forth the subject; it gives us certain pieces of information *about* the subject, through a pre-formulated symbolic notation agreed upon between artist and audience; in this sense it is a linguistic act rather than the embodiment of an experience. For an intelligent exploration of nominalist method in literary criticism, see James Guetti, *The Limits of Metaphor* (Ithaca, 1967). A view of language that is closer to my own is described by Verhaar in his commentary on H. J. Pos (Verhaar, pp. 116–117); and Allen Tate, though for reasons very different from mine, comes to similar conclusions in *The Man of Letters in the Modern World* (Cleveland and New York, 1964), p. 117.

9. P. F. Strawson, *The Bounds of Sense* (London, 1966), p. 273. Cf. Georges Bataille: "Qui saura jamais ce qu'est ne rien savoir?" quoted by Jacques Derrida in *L'Ecriture et la différence*, p. 394, from *Le Petit*, but I do not find it in that work. See also chapter 3, n. 10, below.

On the theme of passivity discussed below, cf. Olga Bernal, *Langage et fiction dans le roman de Beckett* (Paris, 1969), p. 19: "Quand faute de mots on ne peut ni dire ni penser les choses, alors on ne peut précisément que les subir." ("When, for lack of words, one can neither say nor think things, then, precisely, one must suffer them.")

Only recently has some opposition to the exaggerated claims

for the role of language in perception and thought begun to develop. Hans G. Furth, in *Thinking Without Language* (New York and London, 1966), says: "the basic development and structure of the intelligence of the deaf in comparison with the hearing is remarkably unaffected by the absence of verbal language. . . . If then the thinking processes of the deaf can and must be explained without recourse to language, a nonverbal approach to thinking may be a fruitful one for studying thinking in general." (pp. 227–228) In *Piaget and Knowledge: Theoretical Foundations* (Englewood Cliffs, N.J., 1969), Furth repeats: "the basic manifestations of logical thinking in linguistically deprived deaf children were present without any important structural deficiencies." (p. 119) "Thus, having set out to explore the nature of the linguistic contribution to the development of thinking, we found ourselves in the awkward position of having to explain the development of thinking without language." (p. 120) I am grateful to Dr. Daniel Ling of McGill University for referring me to the work of Furth, R. Conrad, and other psychologists who are investigating the non-linguistic aspects of thought.

10. In making this distinction between recent and earlier literature, I find myself in agreement with Gaëtan Picon, *L'Ecrivain et son ombre* (Paris, 1953): "le langage doit maintenant produire le monde qu'il ne peut plus exprimer." ("language must now produce the world which it can no longer express." p. 158), or "L'oeuvre moderne tire de son langage même toute la réalité qu'elle contient." ("The modern work draws from its very language whatever reality it contains," p. 160). On the other hand, Jacques Derrida argues that previous literature could not have simply been chronologically subsequent to experience either, since meaning cannot precede itself (*L'Ecriture et la différence*, pp. 15, 21).

11. See Wayne Shumaker, *Elements of Critical Theory* (Berkeley and Los Angeles, 1952) for a formulation of the opinion to which I object: e.g. p. 13n. For a defence of aesthetics, interpretation, and literary criticism see Picon, chapter VI.

12. Cf. Bashō, *The Narrow Road to the Deep North* (Baltimore, 1966), p. 33: "However well phrased your poetry may

be, if your feeling is not natural—if the object and yourself are separate—then your poetry is not true poetry but merely your subjective counterfeit."

13. There is another well-known passage from Humboldt that is very much to the point:

> Man thinks, feels, and lives only within language, and he must first be taught by language even to understand art, which does not have its effects through language at all. At the same time he senses and knows that language is only a medium, that there is an invisible realm beyond it, in which he hopes to come to be at home, but only through it. Common experience and profoundest thought both bewail the inadequacy of language, and conceive of that region as a distant land, towards which only language leads, and it never quite. (Wilhelm von Humboldt, *Schriften zur Sprach-philosophie*, Stuttgart, 1963, p. 77).

Cf. C. D. Grabbe, *Don Juan und Faust*, II, i:

FAUST: Und warum fühl' ich Durst, mehr zu erfor-
           schen,/Als mir die Sprache bieten kann?
DER RITTER: Weil du/Zu diesem Durst dich künstlich reizest.

(FAUST: And why do I feel thirst to find out more than
           language has to offer?
THE KNIGHT [MEPHISTOPHELES]: Because you stimulate your-
                            self artificially to feel that
                            thirst.)

14. See Gilles Deleuze, *Logique du sens* (Paris, 1969) and recent articles of Badiou and Kristeva.

2. SUBJECT AND OBJECT IN ROMANTIC FICTION

1. Edmund Husserl, *Ideas* (New York, 1962), p. 15.

2. Alfred de Vigny, *Oeuvres complètes* (Paris, 1948), I, 691; II, 973–74, 1312. See also the author's "Contribution of Neurology to the Scepticism of Alfred de Vigny," *Journal of the History of Medicine*, IX (1954), 331–340.

3. F. M. Dostoyevsky, *Biesi* (Berlin, 1921), II, 100.

4. L. N. Tolstoy, *Voina i Mir* (Moscow, 1953), II, 764–65. There is also a specific illustration of the problem in the portrait of the senile Countess Rostova (First Epilogue, Chapter XII).

5. See the author's "A Note on the History of Synaesthesia," *MLN*, LXII (1956), 203–206.

6. Luc de Clapiers, Marquis de Vauvenargues, *Oeuvres complètes de Vauvenargues* (Paris, 1827), I, 77–78; cf. David Hume, *A Treatise of Human Nature* (Oxford, 1941), pp. 413–418. See also Francis Hutcheson, *An Essay on the Nature and Conduct of the Passions and Affections* (Glasgow, 1769), pp. 84 ff., on the reasons for the difficulty of controlling the desires by reason. One wonders whether Hutcheson's discussion of the perverted sense of honor (pp. 89, 98–99, 173) has any bearing on the characterization of Falkland in *Caleb Williams,* though the theme is of course something of a commonplace in eighteenth-century psychology (see for instance Rousseau's essay on the origins of inequality).

7. William Godwin, *Enquiry Concerning Political Justice and Its Influence on Morals and Happiness* (London), 1798, I, xxvi.

8. Ibid., I, 403, 412, 420.

9. Ibid., I, 412. Of course, Godwinian psychology was not the only precursor of Bergsonian *durée* and Proustian memory. Cf. George Berkeley, *A Treatise Concerning the Principles of Human Knowledge,* section 98; and Georges Poulet, *Etudes sur le temps humain* (Paris, 1949), pp. xxx, xxxii. The holistic psychology promoted by associationism is well described by Walter Jackson Bate, *From Classic to Romantic* (Cambridge, Mass., 1949), pp. 119 ff. Launcelot Law Whyte's *The Unconscious before Freud* (New York, 1962) is a useful addition to the bibliographies of eighteenth- and nineteenth-century psychology.

Godwin's insistence on the continuity of consciousness should be compared with its Cartesian analogues (see below). The ground of the problem had shifted in the interval from the continuity of the soul to the continuity of the self. See Hume, *A Treatise of Human Nature,* pp. 251–263; and the reply in Thomas Reid, e.g. *Essays on the Intellectual Powers of Man* (London, 1941), pp. 200–206.

10. Godwin, I, 406; see also Gottfried Wilhelm Leibnitz, *Oeuvres philosophiques de Leibnitz* (Paris, 1900), I, 77–78.

11. Godwin, I, 411–12. The eighteenth century's preoccupation with this problem is well known; for its connections with aesthetics see Albert Funder, *Die Ästhetik des Frans Hemsterhuis und ihre historischen Beziehungen* (Bonn, 1913), pp. 40–43.

12. See William Watson, *A Treatise on Time* (London, 1785), pp. 13–14, 30 ff., 40; and, for general background, David Hartley, *Theory of the Human Mind* (London, 1775), pp. iii–v, 334–346, and William Godwin, *An Enquiry Concerning Political Justice* (Toronto, 1946), III, 7. The state of the will in dreams is discussed by Dugald Stewart in *Elements of the Philosophy of the Human Mind* (London, 1792), pp. 320–339.

13. Cf. Godwin, *Political Justice* (London, 1798), I, 339–401. The French passages from Leibnitz that follow in my text translate: "Therefore it is wise to make a distinction between *perception,* which is the interior state of the monad . . . and *aperception* which is consciousness, or the reflexive awareness of that inner state, and which is not given to all souls, nor at all times to the same soul." "We are never without perceptions, but we are necessarily often without aperceptions . . ." "disquiet . . . which nevertheless often creates our desire and even our pleasure, by lending it a kind of exciting flavor."

14. See the controversy with Gassendi over the state of the soul during lethargy: René Descartes, *Oeuvres* (Paris, 1904), VII, 264, 356–357; and Francisque Bouillier, *Histoire de la philosophie cartésienne* (Paris, 1868), I, 78. Cf. also Berkeley, *Principles,* section 98.

15. "Doctors now play the same role in society that priests did in the Middle Ages . . . The abbé has surrendered his place at the bedside to the physician, as though this society, in turning materialist, had decided that the care of the soul would henceforth have to depend on the cure of the body." Vigny, *Oeuvres complètes,* I, 659. See Jules Barbey d'Aurevilly, *Les Diaboliques* (Paris, Lemerre, n. d.), p. 151, for a very similar remark by Dr. Torty, who seems to be modeled on Dr. Noir.

16. Among the numerous works on the psychological background of English literature are Lawrence Babb's *The Elizabethan Malady* (East Lansing, 1951) and Geoffrey Bullough's *Mirror of Minds* (London, 1962). A forthcoming book by Arthur Efron on *Don Quixote* (University of Texas Press) offers a very different view of Quixote's madness from the one which this essay assumes.

17. It is by now apparent that there is an abundance of subjectivity, sentimentality, and subtle dishonesty in both Meursault and Camus. Still, I believe that it would be as much of a mistake to exclude the elements I have been discussing from an interpretation of the book as to ignore all that is dubious or unsavory about Camus' protagonist.

18. Laurence Sterne, *A Sentimental Journey through France and Italy* (New York, 1926), p. 132. ". . . whatever is my situation, let me feel the movements which rise out of it, and which belong to me as a man—and if I govern them as a good one, I will trust the issues to thy justice: for thou hast made us, and not we ourselves."

19. Rousseau expresses himself in surprisingly similar terms in the *Rêveries* (*Oeuvres complètes* [Paris, 1959], I, 1084–1085).

20. To escape the world with Virgil and Shakespeare *"is not walking in a vain shadow—nor does man disquiet himself in vain by it*—he oftener does so in trusting the issue of his commotions to reason only—" (p. 124).

21. The conclusion of Vigny's *Stello*. All these authors seem to teeter on the edge of an awareness that becomes the positive doctrine (and perhaps the arch-heresy) of Kafka: that love between man and man is impossible. Justice is the only medium through which we may attempt to know other men; love is a posture which is possible only vis-à-vis God.

22. "But the Fille de Chambre hearing there were words between us, and fearing that hostilities would ensue in course . . . had stolen so close to our beds, that she had got herself into the narrow passage which separated them, and had advanced so far up as to be in a line betwixt her mistress and me—

So that when I stretch'd out my hand, I caught hold of the Fille de Chambre's—" Sterne, p. 169.

23. The theme of ambiguity in the novel has received interesting and elaborate treatment since this essay was written. See, for instance, Robert M. Adams, *Strains of Discord* (Ithaca, 1958); René Girard, *Mensonge romantique et vérité romanesque* (Paris, 1961); Angus Fletcher, *Allegory: The Theory of a Symbolic Mode* (Ithaca, 1964); Alan Friedman, *The Turn of the Novel* (Oxford, 1966). The relation between Camus and Sterne was also subsequently discussed in Ernest H. Lockridge, "A Vision of the Sentimental Absurd: Sterne and Camus," *Sewanee Review,* LXXII (1964), 652–657; and the interpretation of Goethe's *Werther* that follows in this chapter was developed in Hans Reiss, "*Die Leiden des Jungen Werthers:* A Reconsideration," *MLQ,* XX (1959), 81–96.

24. Cf. Godwin exonerating the assassin, who "cannot help the murder he commits, any more than the dagger," *Political Justice,* section VII ("Of Crimes and Punishments"); or Vigny, analysing the medical causes of Chatterton's ostensibly Romantic suicide (*Oeuvres complètes*, I, 863).

25. See S. Atkins, "J. C. Lavater and Goethe: Problems of Psychology and Theology in *Die Leiden des Jungen Werthers,*" *PMLA,* LXIII (1948), 520–76.

26. See the discussion of the reasons for Werther's suicide in Gertrud Riess, *Die Beiden Fassungen von Goethes "Die Leiden des Jungen Werthers"* (Breslau, 1924), p. 37; and cf. n. 24, above.

27. I should like to thank Lionel Abel for pointing out the relevance of *Messages* for my argument. The above quotation is from *Messages: première série* (Paris, 1926), pp. 43–44: "Il est certain que le passage du moi au non-moi, le plus important événement peut-être de la vie humaine, ne s'effectue point, à l'origine, par le moyen de l'intelligence claire et distincte, et ne s'explique que par la présence en nous, pour user des termes de Leibnitz, des perceptions confuses de l'univers."

28. Ibid., p. 44. "L'ébauche d'une nature intuitive, intermédiaire entre la réalité et l'idée, et principe essentiel de cette dernière, a été l'oeuvre de ce qu'on appelle *grosso modo* l'impressionisme."

29. Ibid., p. 46: "Rien ne vaut l'impressionisme pour nous faire appréhender la vie dans l'instant qu'elle se fait, *avant* le

contrôle artificiel de la perception et du concept . . ." "Contrôle" might also be rendered "appraisal" or "censorship." (See also M. Merleau-Ponty, *Phénoménologie de la perception* [Paris, 1945], p. xi, and the reference to Reid in n. 9, above.)

30. Ibid., pp. 57–58: "Considérant cette dissolution de l'objet dans notre moi comme le premier temps d'une réadaptation fonctionnelle, il comprend que le second temps consiste dans une affirmation nouvelle de l'objet, basée sur les données de la première expérience passive." Cf. Francis Ponge, *Tome premier* (Paris, 1965), pp. 287–288 (conclusion to "Notes prises pour un oiseau.")

31. These quotations are from C. Cusanus, *The Idiot in Four Books* (London, 1650; San Francisco, 1940), p. 38. "Deus enim est omnium exemplar. Unde, cum omnium exemplar in mente ut veritas in imagine reluceat, in se habet ad quod respicit. . . . Sed in nostris mentibus ab initio vita illa similis est dormienti, quousque admiratione, quae ex sensibilibus oritur, excitetur ut moveatur, tunc motu vitae suae intellectivae in se descriptum reperit quod quaerit. Intelligas autem descriptionem hanc resplendentiam esse exemplaris omnium modo quo in sua imagine veritas resplendet, . . ." Nicolò Cusano, *Scritti Filosofici* (Bologna, 1965), I, 132. See also Ernst Cassirer, *The Individual and the Cosmos in Renaissance Philosophy* (New York, 1963), pp. 123 ff., "The Subject-Object Problem." I am indebted to Frederick Plotkin for pointing out the relevance of this chapter for my topic.

32. *L'Univers imaginaire de Mallarmé* (Paris, 1961), p. 20. ". . . l'aventure intérieure réclame chez lui une *preuve,* qui ne saurait venir que du monde sensible." There is an extraordinary passage (p. 21) on the dual character of the concept itself, only one of whose faces is abstract: "Le concept lui-même vit en nous, il a sens d'abord pour nous qui le pensons; son universalité ne l'empêche pas de s'attacher particulièrement à la réalité la plus intime de chacun et d'en accepter l'empreinte. Sous sa face d'objectivité et de lumière, il possède . . . un 'envers' . . . l'idée' . . . entre donc en connivence avec notre humeur la plus secrète, ce qui lui donne, à elle aussi, une physiologie." ("The concept itself lives in us, it has meaning first of

all for us who think it; its universality does not prevent it from attaching itself to each one's most intimate reality and from taking its imprint. Beneath its face of objectivity and light, it has . . . a 'verso' . . . 'the idea' . . . hence enters into a secret understanding with our most private humor, which gives it too a physiology.")

33. Heinrich von Kleist, *Kleists Aufsatz über das Marionetten-theater* (Berlin, 1967), p. 12: "Doch das Paradies ist verriegelt und der Cherub hinter uns; wir müssen die Reise um die Welt machen, und sehen, ob es vielleicht von hinten irgendwo wieder offen ist."

34. In part II, chapter lxii, of *Don Quixote,* there is a talking head which also has powers of divination.

35. See David O. Evans, "Vigny and the *Doctrine de Saint-Simon,*" *Romanic Review,* XXXIX (1948), 22–29.

36. Vigny, *Journal d'un poète* (Paris, 1867), p. 264. Vigny was perfectly aware of the link between his problem and Cervantes': "In order to write we have to begin by lying to ourselves . . . creating a phantom which we can afterwards adore or profane. . . . So that we are always Don Quixotes, and less excusable than Cervantes' heroes, for we know that our giants are wind-mills and we intoxicate ourselves to persuade ourselves that they are giants." *Journal d'un poète* (Paris, 1935), I, 538.

37. See for instance John Owen, *The Sceptics of the Italian Renaissance* (London, 1893), pp. 186–87; P. O. Kristeller, *Il pensiero filosofico di Marsilio Ficino* (Firenze, 1953), pp. 376–377; and Anthony Levi, *French Moralists* (Oxford, 1964), p. 338. There is also an extensive account of Renaissance scepticism in the early chapters of William Elton, *King Lear and the Gods* (San Marino, California, 1966).

38. For a nineteenth-century instance of this attitude see the interesting quotation from Feuerbach in Jacques Derrida, *L'Ecriture et la différence* (Paris, 1967), p. 19. A more recent example is Walter Ong's *The Presence of the Word.*

39. Cf. Eugen Fink, *Sein, Wahrheit, Welt* (den Haag, 1958), p. 154. See also Hilton Kramer, "Art at the End of Its Tether," *The New York Review of Books,* XI (September 26, 1968), 42–45, and Mikel Dufrenne, *Pour l'homme* (Paris, 1968), p. 73.

3. THE DESCRIPTIVE STYLE:
CHATEAUBRIAND, ROUSSEAU, CAMUS

1. For an earlier version of this passage, see François René de Chateaubriand, *Mémoires de ma vie* (Paris, Wittmann, 1948), ed. Maurice Levaillant, pp. 132–133.

I translate "Mail" in the third paragraph as "drive," though there was apparently no road running through the copse at Combourg that went under the name of "le grand Mail."

2. "S'il est des paysages qui sont des états d'âme, ce sont les plus vulgaires." "If there be any landscapes that are moods, they are the most commonplace." Albert Camus, *Noces* (Paris, 1947), p. 34.

For an interesting discussion of Chateaubriand's personality, see Jean-Pierre Richard, *Paysage de Chateaubriand* (Paris, 1967).

3. I owe part of this observation to Richard Abrams; cf. James Guetti, *The Limits of Metaphor* (Ithaca, 1967), pp. 164 ff. Metaphor arises from the conflict of perceptions, from the clash between what we perceive and what we know, and so subverts classification; pseudo-metaphors such as these merely create an abstract class of non-entity that two percepts supposedly have in common. See my Introduction, above.

Like most of the superfluous parts of this passage in the *Memoirs,* these lines were added in the revision of the manuscript.

4. On the subject of birds, the reader may wish to look at Michelet's *L'Oiseau* and Ponge's "Notes prises pour un oiseau."

5. François René de Chateaubriand, *Les Natchez* (Baltimore, Paris, London, 1932), I, 268.

6. See Introduction, n. 12. The full quotation from Bashō reads: "Go to the pine if you want to learn about the pine, or to the bamboo if you want to learn about the bamboo. And in doing so, you must leave your subjective preoccupation with yourself. Otherwise you impose yourself on the object and do not learn. Your poetry issues of its own accord when you and the object have become one—when you have plunged deep enough into the object to see something like a hidden glimmer-

ing there. However well phrased your poetry may be, if your feeling is not natural—if the object and yourself are separate—then your poetry is not true poetry but merely your subjective counterfeit."

There are resemblances to Schopenhauer's aesthetics in the argument of this chapter and of chapter 5, but they represent confluences rather than influences, as will be apparent from the context of discussion.

7. *The Notebooks of Samuel Taylor Coleridge* (New York, 1957), I, entry 523. For similar observations see Friedrich Schiller's *Über die ästhetische Erziehung des Menschen,* letter twelve and note; also Susan Sontag, 'The Aesthetics of Silence.'

8. Cf. the late afternoon scene in "Le Désert," the last section of Camus' *Noces.*

The question of pre-conscious categories was discussed at the 1969 phenomenological conference in Chicago by Aaron Gurwitsch under the rubric of "proto-logic," "a logicality in the Lebenswelt itself."

9. Adapted from the David Magarshack translation of Nicolai V. Gogol, *Tales of Good and Evil* (New York, 1957), p. 103, with the assistance of Robert Beckwith. Gogol, incidentally, is almost as rich in bird-scapes as is Chateaubriand (see especially *Taras Bulba*) with their function in Robbe-Grillet; and see Sontag (n. 7, above).

Compare the reassuring role of objects in, e.g., *Robinson Crusoe* with their function in Robbe-Grillet.

10. Michael Scott (1798–1835), one of the finest descriptive writers in the language. *Littel's Living Age,* LXXII (January–March 1862), p. 190, says of him: "Mr. Scott saw with an eye of wonderful vividness and insight, but his mind was cool and canny all the time, and hence, perhaps, the wonderful accuracy with which he portrays what he saw. He casts no gleam of poetry round it." A simpler summary of Scott's achievement is implied by the famous line from Nabokov's *The Real Life of Sebastian Knight:* ". . . the heartbreaking beauty of a pebble among millions and millions of pebbles, all making sense, but what sense?" Scott's descriptions, even at their very best, take place in an atmosphere of total neutrality; but there is hardly a page that does not have

its brilliant glassy scenes. Though brief examples do little to convey an impression of style, I give two typical sentences. In *Tom Cringle's Log* (London and New York, 1938), pp. 82–83, the sense of tropical heat is communicated in this way: "There was not a cloud in the heavens, but a quivering blue haze hung over the land, through which the white sugar-works and overseers' houses on the distant estates appeared to twinkle like objects seen through a thin smoke, whilst each of the tall stems of the cocoa-nut trees on the beach, when looked at steadfastly, seemed to be turning round with a small spiral motion, like so many endless screws."

In an earthquake (pp. 103–4), while "the whole brute creation, in an agony of fear, made the most desperate attempts to break forth from their enclosures into the open air, the end wall of my apartment was shaken down: and falling outwards with a deafening crash, disclosed, in the dull grey mysterious twilight of morning, the huge gnarled trees that overshadowed the building, bending and groaning, amidst clouds of dust, as if they had been tormented by a tempest, although the air was calm and motionless as death."

11. H. J. Pos argues similarly on the subject of actions undertaken without conscious motivation: "automatic activities, which are no longer set off by a formulated intention—were these not originally initiated by a formulated intention—and doesn't it still direct unconsciously acts which now are apparently independent of all language? We reply that the operation of language was only provisional and above all that the actions set off by it were only apparently so initiated: in this case language is a stimulant and not a cause, it only outlines acts the meaning of which is known by an experience which is not related to the realm of language." *Keur Uit de Verspreide Geschriften van Dr. H. J. Pos* (Assen, 1957), I, 210: "les manoeuvres automatisées qui ne sont plus déclenchées par une initiative formulée, ne l'ont-elles pas été à l'origine par elle et celle-ci ne dirige-t-elle pas inconsciemment des actes en apparence indépendantes de tout langage? Nous répondrons que le dictat du langage n'a été que provisoire et surtout que les manoeuvres déclenchées par lui ne l'étaient qu'en apparence: ici la parole est un stimulant et non

une cause, elle ne fait que dessiner des actes dont le sens est connu par une expérience qui ne relève pas du domaine de la parole." ("Dictat du langage" is difficult to translate: it might be rendered "directions given by language.") Cf. the chapter "Language Over-rated" in Rudolf Arnheim, *Visual Thinking* (Berkeley and Los Angeles, 1969). Language, in Arnheim's view, "serves as a mere auxiliary to the primary vehicles of thought" (p. 243); and many of the troubles in language develop "because words, as mere labels, try to keep up with the live action of thought taking place in another medium." (p. 245)

An interesting approach to this question is suggested by R. W. Leeper, as quoted in Jerome Bruner, *Studies in Cognitive Growth* (New York, London, Sydney, 1966), p. 21: "Maybe the whole point can be summed up by saying that movements often are like symbols or actually are symbols." See also Introduction, n. 9, above, and M. Merleau-Ponty, *Signes* (Paris, 1960), p. 118. The *Phénomenologië de la perception* (Paris, 1945), p. xi, also deals with the general problem of pre-conscious or unformulated knowledge; cf. Eugene F. Kaelin, *An Existentialist Aesthetic* (Madison, 1962), p. 201, on Descartes.

12. For a more radical rejection of concepts as a key to literature see Georges Bataille, "Méthode de méditation," as well as Maurice Blanchot's *L'Espace littéraire* and *Lautréamont et Sade.*

13. Paris, 1957. See pp. 94–97.

Other interesting approaches to Rousseau have been developed recently, notably by Paul de Man, Barbara Guetti, and Jacques Derrida. But Plotinus also provides an illuminating predictive commentary: see the *Enneads* (London, [1956]), p. 624.

14. "A Tipasa, je vois équivaut à je crois . . . ." *Noces,* p. 21; or, in his notes on the novel, "On ne pense que par images." ("One thinks only in images." *Théâtre; récits; nouvelles* [Paris, 1962], p. 1904).

15. This view of Camus is disputed by Robbe-Grillet in *Pour un nouveau roman,* but in the contrast with Rousseau its relative truth emerges clearly again.

There is an important resemblance between the "others" in Rousseau (and possibly in Camus as well) and Beckett's "they" in *The Unnamable*. See, for instance, *Three Novels by Samuel Beckett* (New York, 1965), p. 353. As in certain parts of the *Rêveries,* the speaker is unable to feel in the supposedly "normal" way; he shows a recurrent tropism toward ataraxia; and "they" attempt to "humanize" him and force a continuity upon him.

16. A typically conventional description can be found in letter 38 of *Julie* (from St. Preux to Julie): "Je trouve la campagne plus riante, la verdure plus fraîche et plus vive, l'air plus pur, le ciel plus serein; le chant des oiseaux semble avoir plus de tendresse et de volupté; le murmure des eaux inspire une langueur plus amoureuse, la vigne en fleurs exhale au loin de plus doux parfums; un charme secret embellit tous les objets ou fascine mes sens; on dirait que la terre se pare pour former à ton heureux amant un lit nuptial digne de la beauté qu'il adore et du feu qui le consume." The last clauses in particular show Rousseau treating the description merely as a stage-setting.

("I find the countryside more smiling, the verdure fresher and more vivid, the air purer, the sky more serene; the song of the birds seems more tender and voluptuous; the murmur of water inspires a more loving languor, the flowering vine breathes at a distance sweeter perfumes; a secret charm beautifies all objects or fascinates my senses; one would say that the earth is adorning itself to create for your happy lover a nuptial bed worthy of the beauty he adores and of the flame that consumes him.")

Even when Rousseau sets about deliberately observing specific objects they sublimate immediately into generalizations: see the *Rêveries* in *Oeuvres complètes* (Paris, 1959), I, 1062–63.

17. For Rousseau even descriptive music must describe our responses to nature, not nature itself. The composer must learn to "rendre du bruit par du chant; . . . s'il faisait coasser des grenouilles, il faudrait qu'il les fît chanter: car il ne suffit pas qu'il imite, il faut qu'il touche et qu'il plaise; sans quoi sa maussade imitation n'est rien . . ." ("to express noise by song; . . . if he wants to imitate the croaking of frogs, he must learn to make them sing: for it is not sufficient to imitate, he must touch and please the listener; without which his dreary imitation is nothing . . ." "Essai sur l'Origine des Langues," chapter xiv).

18. The change from one to the other is described with great accuracy in the section of *Noces* called "Le Vent à Djémila." Man gradually acquires a clear-cut idea of death. "Naturellement, c'est un peu décourageant. Mais l'homme y gagne une certaine familiarité avec le beau visage du monde. Jusque-là, il le voyait face à face. Il lui faut alors faire un pas de côté pour regarder son profil. Un homme jeune regarde le monde face à face." ("Naturally, it's a bit discouraging. But man gains from it a certain familiarity with the beautiful face of the world. Until that time he has seen it only face to face. Then he has to step aside to see it in profile. A young man looks at the world only face to face.")

19. E.g. the early pages of *René:* "Je vois encore le mélange majestueux des eaux et des bois de cette antique abbaye où je pensai dérober ma vie aux caprices du sort; j'erre encore au déclin du jour dans des cloîtres retentissants et solitaires. Lorsque la lune éclairait à demi les piliers des arcadestes, dessinait leur ombre sur le mur opposé, je m'arrêtais à contempler la croix qui marquait le champ de la mort et les longues herbes qui croissaient entre les pierres des tombes." Or, "Tantôt ce même soleil qui avait vu jeter les fondements de ces cités se couchait majestueusement à mes yeux sur leurs ruines; tantôt la lune se levant dans un ciel pur, entre deux urnes cinéraires à moitié brisées, me montrait les pâles tombeaux." And so forth.

("I still see the majestic mingling of waters and woods in that ancient abbey where I thought to rescue my life from the caprices of fortune; I still wander at sunset in the echoing solitary cloisters. When the moon half illumined the pillars of the arches, outlining their shadows on the opposite wall, I would stop to contemplate the cross that marked the field of death and the long grasses that grew between the stones of the tombs."

"Sometimes that same sun which had seen the foundations of these cities laid would set majestically in my view upon their ruins; sometimes the moon rising in a pure sky, between two half broken funeral urns, would light the pale tombs for me.")

20. "Et je suivais tout le long de ce pays quelque chose qui n'était pas à moi, mais de lui, comme un goût de la mort qui nous était commun." ("And I would follow all along that land-

scape something that came not from me, but from it, like a taste of death that we had in common." *Noces,* p. 34). Ultimately Camus is as terrified of nature as Vigny. (*Noces,* p. 98).

4. AN END TO INNOCENCE

1. *Schillers Sämmtliche Werke in Zwölf Bänden* (Stuttgart und Tübingen, 1847), XII, 181: "Sie empfanden natürlich; wir empfinden das Natürliche."

2. See the chapters "Der sich entfremdete Geist; die Bildung" and "Die Welt des sich entfremdeten Geistes," in the *Phänomenologie des Geistes.*

3. J. J. Rousseau, "Discours sur l'origine de l'inégalité parmi les hommes," in *Du Contrat Social* etc. (Paris, Garnier, n. d.), p. 105, n. 1.

4. Jacques Cazotte's "Le Diable amoureux" includes an interesting eighteenth-century analogue to La Motte-Fouqué's theme.

5. *Oeuvres complètes* (Paris, 1875–77), XII, 122, in "Pensées détachées sur la peinture . . . ;" "Le naïf, selon mon sens, est dans les passions violentes comme dans les passions tranquilles . . ."

6. Jakob Boehme, *The Works of Jacob Behmen* (London, 1764), I, 300.

7. Charles Robert Maturin, *Melmoth the Wanderer* (London, 1892), II, 138.

8. "Faut-il brûler Sade," *Les Temps Modernes,* VII (December, 1951), p. 1015. For the purposes of this chapter I have not entered into the more complex aspects of de Sade's work, for which see Blanchot or Foucault.

9. Denis Diderot, *Le Neveu de Rameau* (Genève et Lille, 1950), p. 44. Cf. Georges Bataille, *Le Petit* (Paris, 1963), p. 11.

10. It is possible that this incident is partly apocryphal; but de Sade's biography as a whole is that of someone who, if not conspicuously more dissolute and perverse than some of his contemporaries, was sufficiently so.

On the general theme of the relation of literature to transgression see Georges Bataille, *La Littérature et le mal* (Paris, 1957).

11. *Friedrich Nietzsche: Werke in drei Bänden* (München,

1955), II, 637: "Was aus Liebe getan wird, geschieht immer jenseits von Gut und Böse."

12. Ibid., II, 768: "So dass gerade die Moral die Gefahr der Gefahren wäre?" The English version is from Friedrich Nietzsche, *The Birth of Tragedy and the Genealogy of Morals* (Garden City, New York, 1956), p. 155.

13. Ibid., II, 511: "Ach, wohin ist jene verlogne Unschuld, die ich einst besass, die Unschuld der Guten und ihrer edlen Lügen!" The English for this and the following three quotations is from Friedrich Nietzsche, *Thus Spoke Zarathustra* (Chicago, 1965), p. 283 etc.

14. Ibid., II, 319: "Rate ich euch, eure Sinne zu töten? Ich rate euch zur Unschuld der Sinne . . . . Und wie artig weiss die Hündin Sinnlichkeit um ein Stück Geist zu betteln, wenn ihr ein Stück Fleisch versagt wird." (English edition p. 52).

15. Ibid., II, 294: "Meine Brüder, wozu bedarf es des Löwen im Geiste? Was genügt nicht das lastbare Tier, das entsagt und ehrfürchtig ist? . . . Freiheit sich schaffen und ein heiliges Nein auch vor der Pflicht: dazu, meine Brüder, bedarf es des Löwen . . . . Aber sagt, meine Brüder, was vermag noch das Kind, das auch der Löwe nicht vermochte? Was muss der raubende Löwe auch noch zum Kinde werden?

"Unschuld ist das Kind und Vergessen, ein Neubeginnen, ein Spiel, ein aus sich rollendes Rad, eine erste Bewegung, ein heiliges Ja-sagen." (English edition pp. 22–23).

16. Ibid., II, 401: " 'O Zarathustra, du sollst gehen als ein Schatten dessen, was kommen muss: so wirst du befehlen und befehlend vorangehen.'—

"Und ich antwortete: 'Ich schäme mich.'

"Da sprach es wieder ohne Stimme zu mir: 'Du musst noch Kind werden und ohne Scham.' " (English edition pp. 150–151).

17. Herbert Marcuse, *Eros and Civilization* (Boston, 1955), p. 202.

18. Rousseau, ibid., pp. 62–63.

19. Jean-Paul Sartre, *L'Etre et le néant* (Paris, 1943); see, for instance, the discussion of sincerity on pp. 102–108. A typical comment: "Ainsi, la structure essentielle de la sincérité ne diffère pas de celle de la mauvaise foi . . ." (p. 105: "Thus the essential

structure of sincerity does not differ from that of bad faith
. . .").

20. Fedor Ivanovich Tiutchev; from the lyric beginning "Holy night has arisen."

21. Søren Kierkegaard, *Fear and Trembling and The Sickness unto Death* (Garden City, New York, 1955), p. 108.

5. THE UNCREATING WORD

1. Anthony, Earl of Shaftesbury, *Characteristics* (Indianapolis, New York, 1964), II, 71.
This chapter has several themes in common with Olga Bernal's recent *Langage et fiction dans le roman de Beckett,* and there is an occasional interesting overlap of phrasing despite the differences of literary context. For instance, Bernal describes *Comment c'est* as "un témoignage . . . de l'incréation" (p. 224); and Beckett's chaos, "Ce désert, c'est l'espace, c'est le temps redevenus vides, incréés par le Verbe" (p. 209). ("an instance . . . of uncreation." "This desert is space and time fallen empty again, uncreated by the Word.") See also Gerald L. Bruns' work-in-progress, "Silent Orpheus."

2. ". . . la vérité n'a pas besoin de formules pour exister; elle est liée au réel, qui, lui, par nature est muet." H. J. Pos, *Keur Uit de Verspreide Geschriften van Dr. H. J. Pos* (Assen, 1957), I, 214. Cf. Bernal, ibid., p. 191: "Le monde déverbalisé apparaît comme le seul qui puisse avoir un rapport à la verité." ("The de-verbalized world appears as the only one that can have a relation to truth.")

3. *Of Learned Ignorance* (London, 1954), p. 8. "Sapientissimo Salomone asserente cũctas res difficiles & sermone inexplicabiles . . . Si igitur ita est (ut etiam profundissimus Aristoteles in prima philosophia affirmat) in natura manifestissimis talem nobis difficultatem accidere/ ut nycti coraci solem videre attentati:" *Nicolai Cusae Cardinalis Opera* (Frankfurt, 1962), fo. 1 v.

4. Here I would differ, for instance, with Allen Tate. I do think "incantation" is possible, and that the creation of an imaginary world which has substantial reality is a normal and legitimate activity of poetry: but the reality of the world so

created cannot rest in the words; it must be an experienced phenomenon. I would sooner deny the possibility of re-establishing a sense of contact through words with reality than deny the ability of poetry to invoke or evoke an unknown world.

5. Claude Lévi-Strauss, *La Pensée sauvage* (Paris, 1962), p. 355; Jacques Derrida, *De La Grammatologie* (Paris, 1967), p. 19; Thomas Sebeok, *Animal Communication* (Bloomington, 1968), p. 12. Sometimes the exaggerated claims for language in contemporary philosophy make one think that the Hegelian nightmare has come true, that history is really at an end, and that consciousness believes it has achieved adequacy to all its possible objects. See Lucien Sebag, *Marxisme et structuralisme* (Paris, 1964), pp. 23, 32–36.

6. David Premack and Arthur Schwartz, "Preparations for Discussing Behaviorism with Chimpanzee," in Frank Smith and George A. Miller, *The Genesis of Language* (Cambridge, Mass. and London, 1966), especially the subsection entitled "The Simple Grammars of Simple Worlds," pp. 327–331. See also Noam Chomsky, *Language and Mind* (New York, 1968), pp. 18–19. "The impoverished and thoroughly inadequate conception of language expressed by Whitney and Saussure . . . proved to be entirely appropriate to the current stage of linguistic research. As a result, this conception was held to be vindicated, a not unnatural but thoroughly mistaken conviction. . . . the classical issues have a liveliness and significance that may be lacking in an area of investigation that is determined by the applicability of certain tools and methods, rather than by problems that are of intrinsic interest in themselves."

7. On Rimbaud's dilemma, caught as he was between the effort to erase the hiatus that separates words from things and the compensatory tendency of modern authors to play with the arbitrariness of a language that cannot submit to experience, see Jean-Pierre Richard, *Poésie et profondeur* (Paris, 1955), p. 245, and Yves Bonnefoy, *Rimbaud par lui-même* (Paris, 19[61]), pp. 30–31, 66, 70.

Actually, one might argue that art itself is the proof that language cannot detach itself from its users and become genuinely arbitrary. We know that a line is functioning successfully in a literary work only if it obliges us to assume the position of the speaker; and conversely, in literature, involvement is a prerequisite for the recognition of meaning.

8. Raymond Roussel, *Impressions d'Afrique* (Paris, 1963), p. 68. ". . . Urbain emmena Romulus, qui murmurait encore de vagues réflexions."

9. Interestingly enough, Roussel was an admirer of Jules Verne. On the contemporary crisis in language see the exceedingly interesting passage in Derrida, *De La Grammatologie*, p. 15, as well as the section on p. 18 where he speaks of "Mort de la parole."

10. *Une Saison en enfer*. Cf. Lautréamont, *Poésies*, II: "Les descriptions sont une prairie, trois rhinocéros, la moitié d'un catafalque. Elles peuvent être le souvenir, la prophétie. Elles ne sont pas le paragraphe que je suis sur le point de terminer." ("Descriptions are a meadow, three rhinoceroses, half a catafalque. They may be memory or prophecy. They are not the paragraph that I'm finishing.")

11. "En revenir toujours à l'objet lui-même, à ce qu'il a de brut, de *différent:* différent en particulier de ce que j'ai déjà (à ce moment) écrit de lui." *Tome premier* (Paris, 1965), p. 257. Cf. with my comments on Hopkins in this paragraph Brice Parain, *Petite métaphysique de la parole* (Paris, 1969), p. 73: "Les mots ne sont pas faits pour décrire. Ils ne peuvent pas faire toucher leur objet comme s'il était là. L'homme n'est pas fait, pareillement, pour etre un spectateur. De quoi qu'elle parle, dans une description, il manque toujours la volonté."

The best treatment I know of Hopkins' descriptive style is Dom Anselm Hufstader's "The Experience of Nature in Hopkins' Journals and Poems," *Downside Review*, LXXXIV (April, 1966), 127–149.

12. Michel Foucault, *Les Mots et les choses* (Paris, 1966), p. 302. "On parle parce qu'on agit, et non point parce qu'en reconnaissant on connaît." On the decline in the representative function of language see pp. 249–252.

13. *The Concept of Irony* (London, 1966), p. 289.

14. "Eine solche Art des Ausdrucks, wo das Zeichen ganz in dem Bezeichneten verschwindet . . . ist es, was man in der

Schreibart vorzugsweise genialisch und geistreich nennt." "Uber naive und sentimentalische Dichtung," part I.

15. On the intricate reciprocal influences of photography and the graphic arts see, for instance, Beaumont Newhall, *The History of Photography* (New York, 1964).

16. J. W. Van Dervoort, *The Water World* (New York, etc., 1884), p. 413.

17. On reverie in Howells see the forthcoming paper by William Fischer, "A Fearful Responsibility."

18. Leroy M. Yale, etc., *Angling* (New York, 1897), p. 27. For a text that uses similar rhetorical devices in the description of rivers, though much less successfully, see David Thompson, *The Publications of the Champlain Society: David Thompson's Narrative 1784–1812* (Toronto, 1962). I am indebted to A. J. M. Smith for this reference. The passage on Black River (p. 115) is virtually identical in procedure with the selections from Yale, pp. 90–92, quoted below.

19. Edmund Husserl, *Ideen* . . . (Haag, 1950), I, 194: "Die alte ontologische Lehre, dass die Erkenntnis der 'Möglichkeiten' der der Wirklichkeiten vorgehen müsse, ist . . . eine grosse Wahrheit." Martin Heidegger, *Sein und Zeit* (Tübingen, 1963), p. 38: "Höher als die Wirklichkeit steht die Möglichkeit."

20. *Journals and Papers of Gerard Manley Hopkins* (London, etc., 1959), p. 194.

21. See n. 24, below.

22. *L'expérience intérieure* . . . (Paris, 1954), p. 229. Cf. Samuel Beckett, *Nouvelles et textes pour rien* (Paris, 1958), p. 186: "Bien choisir son moment et se taire, serait-ce le seul moyen d'avoir être et habitat?" ("To choose the right moment and stop talking, is that the only way to have being and a place?")

23. I recognize the verbal analogies to Schelling but I trust what follows will clarify the difference.

24. "At best, the relation of words to their meanings is precarious." Rudolf Arnheim, *Visual Thinking*, p. 245.

25. *L'Ecriture et la différence*, p. 47. "If one must say, with Schelling, that 'everything is Dionysus,' one should know . . . that as pure force, Dionysus is worked through with Difference.

He sees and lets himself be seen." Cf. Cassirer on Ficino's concept of Eros in *The Individual and the Cosmos*, pp. 132–133.

26. ". . . denn das Erkennbare und das Erkennende bestimmen sich je einig in ihrem Wesen aus demselben Wesensgrund. Wir dürfen beides nicht trennen und getrennt antreffen wollen. Das Erkennen ist nicht wie eine Brücke, die irgendwann und nachher zwei an sich vorhandene Ufer eines Stromes verbindet, sondern ist selbst ein Strom, der strömend erst die Ufer schafft und sie ursprünglicher einanderzukehrt, als dies je eine Brücke vermag." Heidegger, *Nietzsche* (Pfullingen, 1961), I, 569–570. Some, like Barthes, would continue to insist that language, not knowledge or perception, is that stream.

27. "Wie, indem die Idee hervortritt, in ihr Subjekt und Objekt nicht mehr zu unterscheiden sind, weil erst, indem sie sich gegenseitig vollkommen erfüllen und durchdringen, die Idee, die adäquate Objectität des Willens, die eigentliche Welt als Vorstellung ersteht; ebenso . . ." etc. Arthur Schopenhauer, *Sämtliche Werke* (Stuttgart/Frankfurt, 1960), I, 259. I am aware of taking a certain liberty in translating "Vorstellung" as Imagination; but in this context it seems to me at least as appropriate as the usual rendering, "idea."

Index